Supporting Students in a Time of Core Standards

NCTE Editorial Board

Supporting Students in a Time of Core Standards

English Language Arts, Grades PreK–2

Susi Long
University of South Carolina

with
William Hutchinson
The University of Michigan

Justine Neiderhiser
The University of Michigan

NCTE National Council of Teachers of English
1111 W. Kenyon Road, Urbana, Illinois 61801-1096

Staff Editor: BONNY GRAHAM

Manuscript Editor: THERESA KAY

Interior Design: JENNY JENSEN GREENLEAF

Cover Design: PAT MAYER

Cover Background: ISTOCKPHOTO.COM/ARTIOM MUHACIOV

NCTE Stock Number: 49409

Library of Congress Cataloging-in-Publication Data

Long, Susi, 1952–
    Supporting students in a time of core standards : English language arts, grades prek–2 / Susi Long with William Hutchinson, Justine Neiderhiser.
        p. cm.
    Includes bibliographical references.
    ISBN 978-0-8141-4940-9 ((pbk))
    1. Language arts (Preschool)--United States. 2. Language arts (Elementary)--United States. 3. Education--Standards--United States. I. Hutchinson, William. II. Neiderhiser, Justine. III. Title.
    LB1140.5.L3L66 2011
    372.6--dc23
                                                            2011038317

Contents

Preface

As a classroom teacher and now as a teacher educator, I believe strongly in protecting the role of teacher as wise and knowledgeable decision maker. Like all educators, I also believe in holding high expectations for every student, which, in their most meaningful form, should be what standards are all about. I worry, however, that standards movements too often result in mandates that constrain rather than support innovative teaching and lead to narrow definitions of what counts as language, literacy, and knowledge. This, in turn, limits possibilities for helping students meet high expectations. So, when I was asked to participate in writing the PreK–2 volume in this series, I was excited to join colleagues who would (a) communicate that a standard should never trump the professional judgment of a wise teacher; (b) convey the need to embrace a diverse range of languages and literacies; (c) send a strong message that standards are not license to mandate specific programs, practices, or curricula; (d) insist on assessments that reflect wise views about how to understand learners and inform instruction; and (e) emphasize that standards should never lead to testing that labels children, teachers, or schools.

I realize, however, that some people will worry that any attention to the new standards will be another element in a slippery slope leading to the imposition of a national curriculum, inappropriate assessment practices, and pay for teachers based on test scores. These are frightening possibilities that reduce teaching to something other than an intellectual act, seriously limiting our ability to support students' success. But this is also the reason I am involved in this project. At the time of this writing, forty-one states have already adopted the Common Core State Standards. Without examples of inspirational teaching that also addresses standards, too many teachers will not realize the tremendous agency (voice and choice) they have, and they will continue to feel constrained. Consequently, we run the real risk that the narrow visions we fear will become the standard. I see a great need for professional literature that highlights *the possible* in a time of standards and includes strategies for addressing interpretations that limit possibilities for teaching and learning. For these reasons, this book is written to support educators (teachers *and* administrators) in continuing to view "teaching as intellectual work" (Nieto, 2003, p. 76), with the assurance that innovative teaching and continuing to build professional knowledge that informs instructional decision making is not only possible but also essential in a time of core standards or any time.

—Susi Long

Acknowledgments

At the heart of any educational text are, of course, students. Their presence in our lives urges us to create spaces where we can grow together by thinking deeply, reflecting critically, and acting purposefully. So it is no surprise that our thanks begin with students. Thank you for sustaining us, challenging us, and inspiring us to do a better job as teachers and as advocates.

Hand-in-hand with thanks to students is, of course, deep gratitude to teachers. Our admiration is beyond measure for teachers' courage to take the kind of stand that makes dynamic teaching possible. In particular, we express profound thanks to the nine teachers highlighted in this book—Janice Baines, Nancy Boggs, Mary Cowhey, Tammy Frierson, Freida Hammett, Jessica Keith, Mariel Laureano, Julia López-Robertson, and Carmen Tisdale. Your generosity in opening your classrooms to the readers of this book is greatly appreciated. We also thank the teacher educators and administrators who brought the work of these great teachers to our attention: JoBeth Allen, Tasha Tropp Laman, Sabina Mosso-Taylor, Sonia Nieto, and Katie Van Sluys.

At NCTE, we thank Kent Williamson, Kurt Austin, and Bonny Graham for supporting the vision that became this series. To Liz Homan at the University of Michigan, we send thanks for excellence in the laborious task of formatting. But it is the endless patience, perseverance, and grace of series editor Anne Ruggles Gere that made this book and series a reality. Anne worked above and beyond the call of duty to ensure that each author was able to express ideas with voice and agency while developing a series that would maintain consistency across texts. We are extremely grateful.

Finally, as with any writing project, it is our family and friends who actually make it possible. They support our vision, and it is *their* endless patience that allows us to make space in our lives to bring each project to completion. We love you and thank you.

—Susi, Justine, and Will

Observing the Common Core State Standards

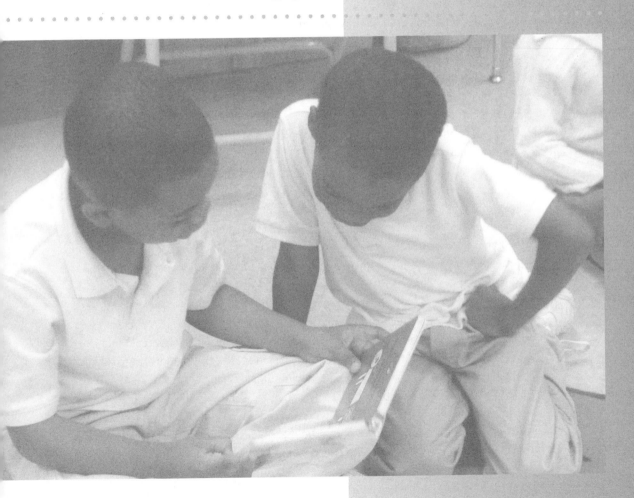

ⓖ Introduction

Not long ago I was driving a van full of youngsters and heard a voice from the back say, "I hate, I hate, I hate the MEAP." (The MEAP is Michigan's state test of math and English language arts [ELA].) I recognized the voice as that of a good student, diligent in every way. Her class had just spent a month preparing for and then taking the MEAP, and she was feeling frustrated by the time spent and anxious about her performance.

That plaintive voice reminded me of concerns I've heard expressed about the latest chapter in the standards movement. The appearance of the Common Core State Standards (CCSS) has aroused a variety of responses, some of them filled with anxiety and resentment. It's easy to get worried about issues of alignment, curricular shifts, and new forms of assessment. And it's frustrating, after carefully developing state ELA standards, to have to put them aside in favor of the CCSS.

Yet, responses to the CCSS have also been positive. Some teachers have said that the grade-specific standards are helpful because they provide useful details about learning goals for students. Others have noted that the CCSS can help them address the needs of transient students because teachers in different schools will be address-ing similar learning goals. Still others have commented that the CCSS can provide a lens through which they can examine their own teaching practices. As one teacher put it, "Looking at the standards made me realize that I wasn't giving much attention to oral language."

In the midst of all these responses stands the reality that the CCSS are now part of the educational landscape. It is also true that these standards do not replace the prin-ciples that guide good teaching. Regardless of new mandates, some things remain constant. One such principle focuses on the fact that teachers think first of their stu-dents, trying to understand their learning needs, developing effective ways to meet those needs, and continually affirming that they are being met. This book, like all four volumes in this series, is written with and by teachers who remain deeply committed to their students and their literacy learning. It is a book addressed to teachers like you.

No one knows as much about your students as you do. You understand the com-munity that surrounds the school and helps to shape their life experiences. You have some information about their family and may even know their parents or guardians personally. You can tell when they are having difficulty and when they are feeling successful. You have watched their body language, scanned their faces, listened to their voices, and read enough of their writing to have some ideas about what matters to them. Your knowledge about your students guides the instructional choices you make, and it shapes your response to any mandate, including the CCSS.

Your knowledge about students is connected to your knowledge of assessment. You have a lot of experience with finding out what students have learned and what they still need to learn. You probably already know about the importance of *authentic assessment*, measures of learning that are connected with work students can be expected to do outside of class as well as in it. No doubt you use formative assessment, measures of learning that give students feedback rather than grades, as a regular part of instruction. For example, you probably make sure that students respond to one another's written drafts as they develop a finished piece of writing. You may have individual conferences with student writers or offer marginal comments and suggestions on their drafts. Or perhaps you meet individually with students to hear them read aloud or tell you about what they have been reading. Whatever type of formative assessment you use, you probably use it to guide instructional choices.

You may have read about the principles for learning adopted by NCTE and other subject-matter associations, principles that position literacy at the heart of learning in all subjects, describe learning as social, affirm the value of learning about learning, urge the importance of assessing progress, emphasize new media, and see learning in a global context. These principles, like others articulated by NCTE, provide a North Star to guide instruction regardless of specific mandates, and you probably recognize, as most accomplished teachers do, that teaching based on such principles will foster student achievement.

Because you are concerned about the learning of *all* of your students, you probably try to find ways to affirm the wide variety of racial, ethnic, socioeconomic, and religious backgrounds that students bring into the classroom. No doubt you are interested in taking multiple approaches to reading, writing, speaking, and listening so that you can engage as many students as possible. Taking this stance convinces you that continual growth and innovation are essential to student achievement, especially when new standards are being introduced.

This book is designed to support you in meeting the challenges posed by the CCSS. It celebrates new visions of innovation and the renewal of long-held visions that may have become buried in the midst of day-to-day obligations. It reinforces a focus on student learning by demonstrating ways of addressing these standards while also adhering to NCTE principles of effective teaching. It does this by, first, examining the CCSS to identify key features and address some of the most common questions they raise. The second section of this book moves into the classrooms of individual teachers, offering snapshots of instruction and showing how teachers developed their practices across time. These classroom snapshots demonstrate ways to address learning goals included in the CCSS while simultaneously adhering to the principles of good teaching articulated by NCTE. In addition to narratives of teaching, this section includes charts that show, quickly, how principles and standards can be aligned. Finally, this section offers suggestions for professional development, both for individuals and for teachers who participate in communities of practice. Thanks to NCTE's Connected Community, you can join in a community of practice that extends across local and state boundaries, enabling you to share ideas and strategies with colleagues from many parts of the country. Embedded throughout this section are student work samples and many other artifacts, and the Connected Community includes many more materials on which you can draw and to which you can contribute. The final section of this book recognizes that effective change requires long-term planning as well as collaboration among colleagues, and it offers strategies and materials for planning units of study articulating grade-level expectations and mapping yearlong instruction.

Voices in the back of your mind, like the "I hate, I hate" voice in the back of my van, may continue to express frustrations and anxieties about the CCSS, but I am confident that the teachers you will meet in this book along with the ideas and strategies offered will reinforce your view of yourself as a professional educator charged with making decisions about strategies and curriculum to advance the learning of your students.

Anne Ruggles Gere
Series Editor

Demystifying the Common Core State Standards

I strongly believe that interpreting standards based on the needs, knowledge, and communities of one's own students is essential. I worry about educators who feel that standards are "the truth, the whole truth, and nothing but the truth." I worry that too many teachers are frightened away from teaching anything that isn't packaged, scripted, mandated, or tested. By telling our own teaching stories, we can empower each other to use standards as points of departure for integrating curriculum, supporting student inquiry, and teaching critically.

—MARY COWHEY, SECOND-GRADE TEACHER

The words of second-grade teacher Mary Cowhey set the tone for the book you are about to read. Like the other early childhood educators who are highlighted in this book, she teaches with deep knowledge of literacy theory and practice (*how* literacy is learned and taught, *what* literate human beings know, and how they *use* that knowledge), confidence in every child, and a commitment to engaging students in ways that motivate, challenge, and lead to achievement. This knowledge and dedication reflects the spirit of new and experienced teachers across the country who have high expectations for their students, but who do not equate those expectations with *standardization* or one-size-fits-all views of teaching and learning. They teach successfully within and beyond standards because they see them as resources to be used in concert with other resources, in particular, their own professional knowledge and commitment to building instruction from the expertise that children bring to their classrooms. They refuse to settle for policies and practices that would have them view students as test scores or that ignore the wealth of cultural resources within and beyond the school walls.

This book is written for new and experienced *teachers, administrators*, and *policymakers* as they work to make this kind of innovative and inspirational teaching a reality in a time of Common Core State Standards (CCSS). We write to *administrators* because we believe that their positions are essential in ensuring the teacher's role as instructional decision maker and in creating school cultures where professional learning and culturally responsive teaching are the norm. We write to *teachers* in support of their commitment to building knowledge and sustaining the innovative spirit that allows them to make a difference for every child. We write to *policymakers* with alternatives to mandating programs because we recognize how easily teachers' confidence and spirit can be taken away when mandates allow little room to use knowledge of theory, practice, and the children in their classrooms.

In a nutshell, we write to remind every educator that *inspirational and innovative teaching in a time of standards is not only possible, it is essential.* Standards need not paralyze us. We can work within and beyond existing systems without compromising great teaching. At the same time, we have a responsibility to take action to change systems (policies, practices, and standards) that oppress inspirational teaching, reduce teaching to skills-only fragments and scripted programs, or lead to labeling students and grading schools and teachers. Thus, while the ultimate goal of this book is to provide ideas and insights about supporting students in a time of core standards, it is also about supporting teachers, administrators, and policymakers in wisely interpreting standards—using them, not being used by them (Mills, 2005)—so they can continue to champion teaching that helps students develop as competent and critical problem solvers who will make a difference in their own lives and the lives of others.

Reading This Book

To accomplish the goals outlined above, this book is organized in three major sections, outlined below.

Section I: Observing the Common Core State Standards

This section provides details about the history and organization of the standards, followed by questions and responses that reflect myths and concerns likely to be raised about the interpretation and implementation of these standards.

Section II: Teachers and Students in Classrooms

Nine early-childhood teachers invite you into their classrooms as they share teaching and learning moments that build from students' strengths, interests, and needs in culturally responsive ways. Each vignette is followed by a description of the teacher's journey toward understanding how to address standards without compromising teaching that makes a difference.

Specific teaching moments are then charted to identify their connections to NCTE principles and beliefs and the Common Core State Standards.

Section III: Planning the Big Picture

In this section, thoughts are shared about how teachers and their administrators might reflect and begin to plan as they consider how to actualize the ideas presented in Sections I and II.

Guiding Principles: Foundations to the Wise Interpretation of Standards

Underlying each section of this book are guiding principles drawn from the expertise of teachers, administrators, and researchers as well as from NCTE principles and beliefs (see Appendix B). These are key concepts that we believe to be foundational to the wise interpretation of standards and to "equity and excellence in education" (Boutte & Hill, 2006). As you read, look for ways that these principles appear in ideas, examples, and resources. These principles define teaching that makes a difference as grounded in commitments to

1. Starting with *the child*

2. *Developing caring relationships* with students and families

3. *Implementing culturally responsive teaching* that

    a. Values and utilizes resources from homes and communities (languages, literacies, worldviews, ways of being) and students' cross-cultural expertise.

    b. Maintains high expectations for every student without standardizing knowledge, children, or approaches to learning.

    c. Develops a critical consciousness by creating opportunities to explore multiple perspectives (voices heard and unheard) as students examine and create texts in pursuit of making a difference for themselves and others.

4. *Assessing knowledge* in ways that are culturally relevant and that inform instruction day-to-day, moment-to-moment

5. *Building professional knowledge* and using that knowledge to generate curriculum, plan for instruction, and effect educational reform

6. *Advocating for educational equity and excellence*

First Steps in Demystifying: Reading the Fine Print

Reading the fine print is important when we encounter any document. This is especially true when interpreting standards. Understanding the fine print means we are more likely to be guided by actual information than by "they say you have to" rumors. A close read of standards and other educational guidelines provides firsthand knowledge so that issues can be addressed if policies and practices reflect partial reads or narrow interpretations. So, in the spirit of reading the fine print, we begin by providing an overview of the Common Core State Standards, their history and content.

Common Core State Standards: Origins and Implementation

The Common Core State Standards for the English Language Arts (ELA) and Mathematics were released in June 2010 after being developed as an initiative of the National Governors Association Center for Best Practices and the Council of Chief State School Officers. Feedback was also provided by members of the National Education Association, the American Federation of Teachers, the National Council of Teachers of Mathematics, and the National Council of Teachers of English, among other organizations. The full texts of the ELA standards, along with other explanatory materials (including the current list of states that have adopted them), are available at http://www.corestandards.org/the-standards/english-language-arts-standards. While these standards are described as having been developed to put authority in the hands of states and school districts, it is important to know that incentives for states to adopt the standards were offered in the form of competitive federal grants. So, while the development of the standards was funded by the governors and state schools chiefs with additional support from the Bill and Melinda Gates Foundation, the Charles Stewart Mott Foundation, and others, there are also connections to federal government initiatives.

In the states that have formally adopted them, the CCSS will replace state standards. States have the right to add 15 percent to them, which means that elements of the state standards could be preserved or new standards could be developed. The timing of implementation varies from one state to the next.

Common Core State Standards: Assessment

In September of 2010, two multi-state consortia, the Partnership for the Assessment of Readiness for College and Careers and the SMARTER Balanced Assessment Consortium, were funded—as a part of the $4.35 billion Race to the Top federal grant program (from the American Recovery and Reinvestment Act of 2009)—to develop assessments to accompany the CCSS. By the time this book is in print, the assessment development phase will be close to completion. Field-testing is scheduled to take place during 2012 and full implementation (in states that have adopted the standards) in 2014. At this point, it is not known what the assessments will look like; preliminary documents indicate that formative as well as summative assessment will play a role, that computers may be involved in both administration and scoring, and that some parts of the assessment, such as writing, may occur over multiple days. For updates on the development of these assessments, check the following websites: http://www.achieve.org/PARCC and http://www.k12.wa.us/SMARTER/default.aspx.

We hope that readers will use the discussion of assessment in this book, as well as in other resources, to consider what needs to happen in their schools, districts, and states so that assessments will be locally determined, culturally and linguistically appropriate and supportive, and focused primarily on assessments that inform day-to-day instruction, without dictating, constraining, or leading to the labeling of students or the grading of teachers and/or schools.

Common Core State Standards: Content and Organization

In a nutshell, the ELA standards address four basic areas for K–2: Reading, Writing, Speaking and Listening, and Language. These areas are proposed as an *integrated model of literacy*. There is no advocacy for separating them instructionally. The intent is that they should be fluidly interwoven throughout the school day.

At first glance, the organization of the CCSS document seems complex, but if you cut to the chase, it can be pretty easy to understand and to put into perspective as one of many educational resources. Viewed in this way, you should be confident in continuing to teach in ways that are the most effective for *you and your students*.

A brief explanation: Each area (Reading, Writing, Listening and Speaking, and Language) is organized into categories. For example, under *Writing*, the categories are (a) text type and purposes, (b) production and distribution of writing, (c) research to build and present knowledge, and (d) range of writing. This is where the standards are found. First there are Anchor Standards. These are merely overarching standards that cross grade levels, K–12. Each anchor standard is broken down into specifics for each grade level (see an example in Figure 1.1, which outlines two of the anchor standards for writing in K–2). The idea is that knowledge about a skill or idea builds from one year to the next. We know that knowledge is never acquired in such a linear fashion, so, as always, teachers will plan for instruction that takes into account the recursive nature of learning. In other words, skills, strategies, and content are revisited in new ways throughout the school day, the academic year, and from year to year.

Writing: Production and Distribution of Writing			
K–5 Anchor Standards for This Category	**How the Anchor Standard Looks in Kindergarten**	**How the Anchor Standard Looks in Grade 1**	**How the Anchor Standard Looks in Grade 2**
Develop and strengthen writing as needed by planning, revising, editing, rewriting, or trying a new approach.	With guidance and support from adults, respond to questions and suggestions from peers and add details to strengthen writing as needed.	With guidance and support from adults, focus on a topic, respond to questions and suggestions from peers, and add details to strengthen writing as needed.	With guidance and support from adults and peers, focus on a topic and strengthen writing as needed by revising and editing.
Use technology, including the Internet, to produce and publish writing and to interact and collaborate with others.	With guidance and support from adults, explore a variety of digital tools to produce and publish writing, including in collaboration with peers.	With guidance and support from adults, use a variety of digital tools to produce and publish writing, including in collaboration with peers.	With guidance and support from adults, use a variety of digital tools to produce and publish writing, including in collaboration with peers.

FIGURE 1.1: Sample anchor standards for writing, K–2.

Interpreting the Fine Print: Myths, Questions, Concerns, and Advice

It is easy to look at any standards document and develop narrow visions for what is possible in the classroom. However, much of that has to do with the way that standards are interpreted and the myths or rumors that tend to develop as a result. Every teacher and administrator knows how important it is to interrupt those myths. You know the kind of myths we're talking about; they usually start with "They say you have to" or "You aren't allowed to." Again and again, we hear about new and experienced teachers losing their creative drive or leaving the profession altogether because they feel bombarded with "They say you have to" directives that contradict their hard-earned professional knowledge (Long et al., 2006; Meier, 2002). Often, those directives turn out to be myths perpetuated because of misinterpreted administrative suggestions, unquestioned traditions, or unfounded rumors. And sometimes directives are real and need to be evaluated and addressed. So the first step in interpreting the fine print of any set of standards means getting to the bottom of comments such as "They say you can only teach Language Arts from 9:00 to 10:30" or "We're not allowed to read aloud more than ten minutes" or "You have to use these books."

The following pages are organized around key questions that reflect these kinds of myths, as well as questions that reflect important issues raised in a time of standards. The purpose is to prevent narrow or inaccurate interpretations of the Common Core

State Standards by describing their open-ended nature and assurance of professional autonomy. The responses to myths and questions also include ideas, insights, and resources for further study.

Are standards intended to be a curriculum, *the* curriculum?

No. This is a perfect example of the importance of reading the fine print. The CCSS are not *the* curriculum or even *a* curriculum. The language of the standards materials makes it clear that "teachers will continue to devise lesson plans and tailor instruction to the individual needs of the students in their classrooms." This means that mandating packaged curricula and scripted programs is not an appropriate response to standards. As you will see in the classroom examples later in the book, teachers can easily meet standards while maintaining the autonomy to create curriculum by drawing on and deepening knowledge of their children, theory, and practice. To put standards in perspective with regard to teacher autonomy, it may be helpful to keep a few key phrases from the Common Core in mind:

"Standards are not a curriculum."

"Standards do not tell teachers how to teach."

"Standards are a first step."

"Skills in these areas should not be handled in isolation."

"Standards are not the only thing that is needed for our children's success."

Will my curriculum be narrowed?

No. There is nothing in the Common Core State Standards that mandates narrowing curriculum from teachers' visions for what will engage, intrigue, and fascinate students. *However*, it is important to be alert to interpretations of standards that may lead to narrower views. Too often, when interpreted through a narrow lens, curriculum focuses on discrete and isolated skills and restricted content. Requirements begin to appear that lead to curricular cloning from classroom to classroom. Student interests, prior knowledge, and cultural relevance are too easily pushed to the back burner or ignored altogether and "student-centered teaching . . . go[es] by the wayside" (Sleeter & Cornbleth, 2011, p. 58). This, in turn, has a profoundly negative effect on student learning and teacher morale (Nieto, 2003). It is important to remember that, just as these standards are not a curriculum, they do not dictate breadth of curriculum or the means by which teachers support student learning. The standards materials make it clear that teachers determine what, when, and how to teach, making individual decisions about the materials they use, the students they target, and the duration of each lesson.

What's the relationship between the Common Core State Standards and my state's standards?

There may well be some overlap between the Common Core State Standards and the standards developed by your state, particularly when you look at the more global goals of the Anchor Standards. Also, states adopt the CCSS with the agreement that it is possible to supplement them with up to 15 percent of state standards. So, some state standards may be preserved, but it is likely that these new standards will replace existing ones.

The Common Core State Standards include lists of *exemplar texts*. Do I have to use them?

No. The word *exemplar* should not be interpreted to mean "required." Exemplar texts are offered as *suggestions* for the kinds of topics and genres that teachers *might* include in their teaching. For example, one list of exemplar texts is organized under the heading "Staying on Topic within a Grade and Across Grades: How to Build Knowledge Systematically in English Language Arts." These titles are used as examples to suggest how teachers can cluster reading around a specific topic so that students can build content knowledge while they are developing as readers. This *in no way implies* (a) that the suggested books are required reading or (b) that students at one grade level should not read texts suggested for students at another grade level.

How might teachers select texts that are appropriate for their students? First, it is important for administrators and policymakers to trust teachers' judgment as they select texts based on their knowledge of each child and culturally responsive literacy theory and practice. At the same time, administrators and teachers will want to access high-quality resources to support their ever-growing knowledge about text selection.

Many teachers also find success creating texts for and with their students. In Section II of this book, you will read about first-grade teacher Janice Baines, who develops books for her classroom that are culturally relevant and therefore immediately compelling and motivating. For example, she began last year by creating a book based on a pop-culture song familiar to her students. To the rhythms of "Pretty Boy Swag" (Soulja Boy, 2010), Janice wrote new words to create "I Can Read Swag." The lyrics were printed and bound in individual books for use during Independent Reading and small-group instruction and projected on the SMART Board for large-group shared reading. She used the books to help children develop fluency while learning about word patterns and high-frequency words among a range of other literacy skills. "I Can Read Swag" was not an exemplar text on any list of suggested books, but it reached students because it was relevant for this particular group of children and it possessed characteristics of texts that meet the needs of emergent readers because it was

- Culturally authentic (Fox & Short, 2003) and relevant (Gay, 2011);

- Predictable and repetitive without dumbing down language, style, or content;

- Filled with high-frequency words and words with simple patterns, as well as more complex vocabulary within naturally flowing text; and

- Supported with illustrations that connected directly to the text and reflected the students' communities and backgrounds.

Above all, "I Can Read Swag" captured students' interest and excitement. They *connected with it* and were therefore motivated to *learn through it*. Janice created "Swag" for the same reasons that she chooses trade books and leveled texts—because she knows her students and she knows what speaks to them and reflects their worlds (Bishop, 2007; Short, 1997)—key pieces of advice in the selection of any texts for classroom use.

The Common Core State Standards use the term *text complexity.* What does that mean and how does it affect my selection of books?

Text complexity is defined by the CCSS as having to do with "level of meaning, structure, language conventionality and clarity, knowledge demands,

> **Resources for Selecting Texts That Meet the Needs of *Your* Students**
>
> *Beyond Leveled Books: Supporting Early and Transitional Readers in Grades K–5* (Szymusiak, Sibberson, & Koch, 2008)
>
> "Books by Faith Ringgold": a list of books by artist and author Faith Ringgold http://www.faithringgold.com/ringgold/books.htm
>
> *Evaluating Children's Books for Bias* http://www.intime.uni.edu/multiculture/curriculum/children.htm
>
> *Free within Ourselves: The Development of African American Children's Literature* (Bishop, 2007)
>
> *Literary Pathways: Selecting Books to Support New Readers* (Peterson, 2001)
>
> *Literature and the Child* (Galda, Cullinan, & Sipe, 2010)
>
> *Literature as a Way of Knowing* (Short, 1997)
>
> "Nine Ways to Evaluate Children's Books that Address Disability as Part of Diversity" http://www.circleofinclusion.org/english/books/section1/a.html
>
> *Postmodern Picture Books: Play, Parody, and Self-Referentiality* (Sipe & Pantaleo, 2008)
>
> *Reading Globally, K–8: Connecting Students to the World through Literature* (Lehman, Freeman, & Scharer, 2010)

word frequency, sentence length [all in the context of] student knowledge, motivation, and interest." While this sounds rather complicated, the intent is simply to ensure that students read increasingly more complex texts as they grow as readers. While text complexity formulas abound, the authors of these standards explain that actual complexity can only be determined when teachers use "their professional judgment, experience and knowledge of their students and the subject." We suggest that you consider the following critical issues when using professional judgment regarding text complexity.

First, while early emergent readers certainly benefit from reading less complex texts (texts with controlled vocabulary, patterns, repetition, and predictability), when simplicity is the only criteria, books may fail to provide support for literacy learning because they do not engage, fascinate, or reflect the worlds of students who are asked to learn through them. In studies of books written specifically to have simple structures, researchers and teachers alike found that many books tend to lose those essential characteristics (Szymusiak, Sibberson, & Koch, 2008). In collections of leveled texts, for example, we still see few authentically portrayed children of color, families with two moms or two dads, or families who speak languages other than English. The activities represented in those texts tend to focus more on middle-class ways of being than on other elements of the rich mosaic that is our society. So, it is important to understand that structurally complex texts may actually be less difficult than books with simple text *if* the reader perceives the content, language, and structure to be familiar and compelling. In other words, complexity "has as much to do with the match between the content of the book and [students'] own experiences as it does with the linguistic difficulty of the book" (Short, 1997, p. 15).

Another point to consider is that readers do not progress through increasingly complex texts in a linear fashion. When children have opportunities to self-select books, they typically move back and forth on their own between easy and difficult texts (Fresch, 1995). Every teacher knows a child like the proud kindergartner who carries a dog-eared copy of *Harry Potter* or the first grader who is motivated to learn more about reading through a love of books that are personally compelling but may have dense text. The same children, in other moments, will engage with equally compelling simpler texts—those that are repetitive and predictable. Wise teachers provide opportunities for children to balance their reading lives by choosing books that reflect a range of complexities for a range of purposes.

What about informational texts?

The Common Core State Standards pay particular attention to informational texts, not only with regard to social studies, science, and technological standards but also in standards for the English language arts. This is consistent with early childhood teachers' use of all kinds of nonfiction texts—picture books, maps, brochures, guidebooks, newspapers, and websites—to support science explorations, mathematical inquiries, and social studies investigations while teaching students how to read and write informational texts.

Several teachers whose classrooms are highlighted in Section II of this book describe how they use informational texts for content learning and as models for student writing. For example, Mariel Laureano uses the book *What Do You Do with a Tail Like This?* to help her kindergartners learn about writing descriptive texts. Freida Hammett uses the *National Audubon Society Field Guides* as her students learn and write about the insects and butterflies they care for in their classroom. Mary Cowhey supports her second graders as they examine and write about issues of social justice using books such as *Harvest Hope*, the biography of Cesar Chavez. In each case, teachers select nonfiction texts that meet the needs of their students and the curriculum they have created for and with them.

Resources for Selecting Nonfiction Books
"Boston Globe—Horn Book Awards for Excellence in Children's Literature" http://www.hbook.com/bghb/current.asp
Is That a Fact? Teaching Nonfiction Writing K–3 (Stead, 2001)
"NCTE Orbis Pictus Award for Outstanding Nonfiction for Children" http://www.ncte.org/awards/orbispictus
Nonfiction Craft Lessons: Teaching Information Writing K–8 (Portalupi & Fletcher, 2001)
Nonfiction Mentor Texts: Teaching Informational Writing through Children's Literature, K–8 (Dorfman & Cappelli, 2009)
A Place for Wonder: Reading and Writing Nonfiction in the Primary Grades (Heard & McDononough, 2009)

Just as with other text lists in the Common Core State Standards, the nonfiction exemplars are intended to be merely suggestions. Numerous resources can be accessed for information about where to find high-quality informational texts and ideas for using them to support content learning and teaching students about nonfiction writing.

What about English language learners?

The Common Core State Standards provide little information with regard to teaching English language learners. In fact, the statement is made that it is "beyond the scope of the Standards to define the full range of supports appropriate for English language learners." However, a significant guiding principle that *is* reflected in the Common Core materials is the importance of supporting students in maintaining home languages while adding

English to their language repertoires. The CCSS explain that "students must be able to use formal English in their writing and speaking, but they must also be able to make informed, skillful choices among the many ways to express themselves through language." This provides clear support for schools as they help students draw from home languages *and* English as educational resources in the classroom.

A common misperception is that young children are confused by the introduction of more than one language when, in fact, the positive cognitive impact of exposure to multiple languages is tremendous and children quickly sort out when and how to use languages in appropriate contexts. When home languages, as well as English, are valued and utilized, all children benefit. English-only students learn about other languages and they learn that their language is one of many ways to communicate in the world. Emerging bilinguals see themselves, their families, their heritage, and their language as positive contributions to the classroom and to society; they have more opportunities to take on the role of expert in the classroom; and they are able to draw on home language resources to support the development of English language proficiency. At the same time, all students have opportunities to develop greater awareness of linguistic structures and cultural usage.

In terms of text selection, emerging bilinguals, like all students, are supported by texts that reflect their worlds, tell compelling stories, have supportive picture-text matches, utilize familiar and natural language, and depict culturally relevant experiences (Freeman & Freeman, 2011). Primary resources for finding supportive texts are the students and their families who are likely to have access to magazines, newspapers, faith-based texts, letters from family members, and so on. Family members can also work with teachers to *create* bilingual texts using students' home languages and English. Creating and/or purchasing bilingual picture books and nonfiction texts can contribute significantly to literacy learning for all children. Language groups and associations in every town and city are also excellent sources, and there are numerous websites that lead teachers to high-quality texts to support students' growing knowledge.

Resources for Selecting Bilingual Children's Books

Bilingual Books for Kids
  http://www.cincopuntos.com

Book by Yuyi Morales and links to websites of other authors http://www.yuyimorales.com

Bookjoy, bilingual books by Pat Mora
  http://www.patmora.com

Monica Brown: Children's Book Author
  http://www.monicabrown.net/

National Association for Bilingual Education
  http://www.nabe.org

National Association for Multicultural Education
  http://www.nameorg.org

Teachers of English to Speakers of Other Languages
  http://www.tesol.org

"Tomás Rivera Mexican American Children's Book Award Winners" http://www.education.txstate.edu/c-p/Tomas-Rivera-Book-Award-Project-Link/Winners.html

---

Several of the classrooms highlighted in Section II of this book provide examples of teachers embracing and using multiple languages even when they may not speak those languages themselves. Tammy Frierson invites language lessons in Hebrew and in Spanish as she learns with her preschoolers about both languages. Julia López-Robertson writes about bilingual literature discussions in second grade. In Jessica Keith's first-grade classroom, students learn about reading and writing in their home languages, adding English to their repertoire. The texts listed in the marginal textbox provide further resources to help teachers and administrators as they work together to understand more about teaching and learning in classrooms where multiple languages contribute to every student's cognitive, linguistic, and cultural development.

What about supporting speakers of African American Language?

Intentional teaching about the legitimacy of African American Language (AAL) and the act of translation (rather than correction) between Standard English (SE) and AAL have been shown time and again to effectively support students both in using their home language and in adding proficiency in SE to their language repertoire (Boutte, 2007; Smitherman, 2006). However, just as English language learning is not addressed in these standards, neither is the teaching of speakers of African American Language.

AAL has long been recognized as a rule-governed, history-rich language and was formally sanctioned as a language by a 1997 resolution of the Linguistic Society of America. Consequently, there are numerous resources to support teachers in helping students explore contrasts, comparisons,

---

Resources for Supporting Emerging Bilingual Students (English Language Learners)

Affirming Students' Right to Their Own Languages: Bridging Language Policies and Pedagogical Practices (Scott, Straker, & Katz, 2008)

Children, Language, and Literacy: Diverse Learners in Diverse Times (Genishi & Dyson, 2009)

Educating Emergent Bilinguals: Policies, Programs, and Practices for English Language Learners (García & Kleifgen, 2010)

Explorations in Language Acquisition and Use (Krashen, 2003)

Latino Children Learning English: Steps in the Journey (Valdés, Capitelli, & Alvarez, 2011)

The Light in Their Eyes: Creating Multicultural Learning Communities (Nieto, 2010)

"NCTE Position Paper on the Role of English Teachers in Educating English Language Learners (ELLs)" http://www.ncte.org/positions/statements/teacherseducatingell

Negotiating Language Policies in Schools (Menken & García, 2010)

Room for Talk: Teaching and Learning in a Multilingual Kindergarten (Fassler, 2003)

Speaking in Tongues, a documentary following four bilingual children http://www.speakingintonguesfilm.info

Words Were All We Had: Becoming Biliterate against the Odds (Reyes, 2011)

Writing between Languages: How English Language Learners Make the Transition to Fluency, Grades 4–12 (Fu, 2009)

Resources for Learning about African American Language

Code-Switching: Teaching Standard English in Urban Classrooms (Wheeler & Swords, 2006)

The Skin That We Speak: Thoughts on Language and Culture in the Classroom (Delpit & Dowdy, 2008)

Spoken Soul: The Story of Black English (Rickford & Rickford, 2000)

"Teaching Students Who Speak African American Language (AAL): Expanding Educators' and Students' Linguistic Repertoire" (Boutte, 2007) in Brisk's *Language, Culture, and Community in Teacher Education*

Word from the Mother: Language and African Americans (Smitherman, 2006)

and historical and global connections between AAL and other languages. Again, teachers and administrators will need to access those resources as they study how to incorporate the art of translation and the study of African American Language structures and history into their classrooms.

How can I help students maintain home cultural identities *and* succeed in the dominant culture when standards do not encompass cultural and cross-cultural competencies?

A concern voiced frequently is that standards will lead to a homogenization of students through one-size-fits-all pedagogies that reduce student identities to that of one cultural model. Standards, and the assessments that typically accompany them, seem to provide no space for valuing students' impressive abilities to succeed within and across cultural and linguistic contexts. Too often, we see students' positive home and community identities compromised or even erased because of narrow interpretations of what constitutes the norm. So the question of maintaining the rich cultural identities of each child's family and community is an important one: How do teachers maintain high expectations for students to achieve within existing power structures (public school education, higher education, business) without standardizing "to the point that one cultural or linguistic group internalizes that their ways of being in the world are better or worse than any other" (Campano, 2007, p. 54)?

Resources for Understanding Culturally Relevant Pedagogies

"African American Communities: Implications for Culturally Relevant Teaching" (Boutte & Hill, 2006)

Change Is Gonna Come: Transforming Literacy Education for African American Students (Edwards, McMillon, & Turner, 2010)

Classroom Diversity: Connecting Curriculum to Students' Lives (McIntyre, Roseberry, & González, 2001)

Culturally Responsive Teaching: Theory, Research and Practice (Gay, 2011)

The Dreamkeepers: Successful Teachers of African American Children (Ladson-Billings, 2010)

Literacy in the Welcoming Classroom: Creating Family-School Partnerships That Support Student Learning (Allen, 2010)

Reading Instruction for Diverse Classrooms: Research-Based, Culturally Responsive Practice (McIntyre, Hulan, & Layne, 2011)

We believe that teachers and administrators can think about this by embracing basic tenets of *culturally relevant pedagogies*. Culturally responsive pedagogies are those that teach "to and through the strengths of the students" (Gay, 2011, p. 31). They are grounded in a commitment to promoting social consciousness and academic achievement by acknowledging "the legitimacy of the cultural heritages of different ethnic groups . . . as worthy content to be taught in the formal curriculum" (p. 32). At the same time, culturally responsive teaching ensures that every student acquires expertise in the "conventions, norms, language codes, and practices within a mainstream" culture (Edwards et al., 2010, p. 46). In other words, while creating classrooms that broaden views of what counts as the norm and making a place for teaching and assessing that values a range of cultural and cross-cultural competencies, culturally relevant teachers ensure that every student can succeed—not just minimally, but brilliantly—within and beyond the existing system. The goal is to create more equitable opportunities for achievement and to support all students in gaining appreciation for the expertise that they and every other student bring to the classroom. In Section II of this book, each classroom example has been carefully selected to highlight strategies for culturally responsive teaching. Further resources can be found in the marginal textbox.

Where is there room for children's play in these standards?

For years, early childhood educators have decried the disappearance of play in classrooms for young children (Ohanian, 2002). Often, standards movements put such a focus on the mechanics of content and skill learning that the playful nature of children's work is neglected. As a consequence, interpretations of standards have often led to a reduction in opportunities for play or playful activities.

Resources for Understanding the Importance of Play
A Child's Work: The Importance of Fantasy Play (Paley, 2004)
The Classrooms All Young Children Need: Lessons in Teaching from Vivian Paley (Cooper, 2009)
Literacy through Play (Owocki, 1999)
What Happened to Recess and Why Are Our Children Struggling in Kindergarten? (Ohanian, 2002)

At the same time, a large body of research demonstrates that intentionally structured environments that include opportunities to play with language and literacies can be highly supportive of literacy learning (Dyson, 2003; Lindfors, 2008; Owocki, 1999; Paley, 2004). As teachers and administrators address standards, it is essential to ensure that "opportunities for play are not diminished and are just as critical as any other standard in early childhood literacy education" (Genishi & Dyson, 2009, p. x). A wide variety of resources are available to support educators in understanding not only the importance of play but also what it looks like in environments where teacher intentionality is key to student success. Again, while the CCSS are not explicit in discussing play as a learning strategy, they do remind educators that decisions for how they will create and carry out curriculum are left up to the knowledgeable teacher.

What about assessment?

We don't yet know what the Common Core assessments will look like, but as you discuss assessments in your schools and districts, we hope you will keep some important issues in mind. First, every teacher knows that recent

**Resources for Assessment
That Informs Instruction**

*Becoming Writers in the Elementary Classroom:
Visions and Decisions* (Van Sluys, 2011)

"Broadening Visions of What Counts: Assessment
as Knowing and Being Known" (Long &
Sibberson, 2005)

*Cultural Validity in Assessment: Addressing Linguistic
and Cultural Diversity* (Basterra et al., 2011)

*Kidwatching: Documenting Children's Literacy
Development* (Owocki & Goodman, 2002)

Knowing Literacy: Constructive Literacy Assessment
(Johnston, 1997)

*The Marriage of Reading Assessment and Instruction:
Stories from Artful Teachers* (Stephens, in press)

NCTE's "Standards for the Assessment of Reading
and Writing" http://www.ncte.org/standards/
assessmentstandards

NCTE's "21st Century Curriculum and Assessment
Framework" http://www.ncte.org/positions/
statements/21stcentframework

"Refocusing on Assessment" (Enciso et al., 2009)

standards movements led to a huge emphasis on high-stakes tests—large-scale standardized tests—that have little to do with the day-to-day needs of children in the classroom. Summative, rather than formative, they are not useful to teachers in terms of informing instruction. In fact, they often do more harm than good as students, teachers, and administrators are pressured to focus on test preparation rather than on teaching students to comprehend and generate complex ideas and solve problems by learning to think critically. Sadly, scores from these tests are often used in ways that punish and humiliate students, teachers, and schools, obviously counterproductive to teaching that makes a difference.

It is also important to think about ways that high-stakes testing can "exacerbate differential access to curriculum—while creating more inequitable conditions in local schools" (Darling-Hammond, 2010, p. 167). Put simply, this means that most standardized tests lead to "enlarging class and race distinctions" (Campano, 2007, p. 146), rather than closing gaps in achievement. When students perform poorly on high-stakes tests, they are labeled in ways that are difficult to shake as they make their way from the kindergarten classroom through high school and beyond. While teachers know that many students' failure on such tests actually reflects the failure of tests to capture what students know, test results continue to take their toll in terms of students' future opportunities for learning. Instruction for students with lower scores often becomes confined to a focus on isolated skills rather than learning skills through the investigation of complex problems and reading and writing for a variety of audiences and purposes, while students who score well enjoy the range of intellectual challenges in their studies.

But it is not just summative assessments that have caused consternation. Assessments developed to inform moment-to-moment instruction have also been used in punitive ways, as class scores are paraded in faculty meetings, on school walls, and in local newspapers. This solves no problems and, in fact, creates new ones as teachers, parents, and children become fearful, stressed, and competitive to the point of missing the purpose of education altogether.

Finally, it is important to understand that the notion of using assessments to provide school-to-school or state-to-state continuity is seriously flawed. The assumption that there can be such continuity leaves out the fact that we are talking about uniquely capable human beings who are defined by more than a test score. This apples-to-apples approach leaves out the rich range of competencies, histories, languages, experiences, and styles that students bring to us and that a teacher can only understand by getting to know a student well. A test score or reading level cannot communicate the child's frame of mind or health on the day of the test, expertise in arenas outside the assessment, relationship with the teacher, or comfort with the testing genre.

These are important issues to consider as the yet-to-be finalized Common Core assessments begin to appear. Initial materials describe the projected assessments as focusing on "actionable data that teachers can use to plan and adjust instruction." This suggests that formative assessment (assessment *for* learning rather than assessment *of* learning) is a part of the plan. This is good news, but we have little idea about just what those assessments will look like and how they will be implemented. Thus, it will be important for teachers, administrators, and policymakers to access high-quality resources and ensure that assessments (a) support responsibly autonomous teaching; (b) do not lead to scripted programs or narrow curriculum; (c) promote appreciation for students' cultural, linguistic, and cross-cultural skills and knowledge; (d) acknowledge that there is much more to know about a child than any one assessment can reveal; and (e) *do not label children or grade teachers or schools.*

Assessment and English Language Learners. Children who are emerging bilingual or multilingual speakers of English *and* their home language(s) exhibit tremendous expertise. Yet this expertise is rarely valued in standards, and therefore it does not appear in the assessments that accompany them. As a result, "without a mechanism for recognizing such intellectual skills as mastering two languages or successfully negotiating differing home, school, and neighborhood environments, the standards-based movement denies the value of some skills that actually support academic achievement" (Hamann, 2008, p. 100).

To address this issue, educators need access to high-quality resources to help them understand strategies for most effectively and *fairly* assessing developing bilingual students. One such resource is the National

Association for the Education of Young Children's 2009 *Supplement on Screening and Assessment of Young English-Language Learners* (http://www .naeyc.org/positionstatements/cape). This document communicates the importance of assessing children by giving great emphasis "to the alignment of assessment tools and procedures with the specific cultural and linguistic characteristics of the children being assessed" (p. 1). Further resources include Basterra et al.'s (2011) *Cultural Validity in Assessment* and the assessment section in Samway and McKeon's (2007) *Myths and Realities: Best Practices for English Language Learners.*

<table>
<tr><td>

Resources for Thinking about Children with Special Needs

"Addressing the Disproportionate Representation of Culturally and Linguistically Diverse Students in Special Education through Culturally Responsive Educational Systems" (Klingner et al., 2005)

From Disability to Possibility: The Power of Inclusive Classrooms (Schwarz, 2006)

"Including Students with Special Needs in a Writing Workshop" (Fu & Shelton, 2007)

"A Pedagogy of Control: Worksheets and the Special Needs Child (Lesley, 2003)

"Special Education: Promises and Problems" (Pardini, 2002)

Yes They Can: Special Needs Students and 21st Century Literacies (Garcia & Chiki, 2010)

</td></tr>
</table>

What do the standards say about students with special needs?

The Common Core State Standards include little about children with special needs, although there is some emphasis on an inclusion model that does not isolate students from mainstream classrooms. The recommendation is to interpret the standards in ways that allow for the "widest possible range of students to participate fully from the outset [with] appropriate accommodations to ensure maximum participation of students with special education needs." With only limited guidance for implementing the standards with students with special needs, schools will need to access high-quality resources to ensure that appropriate expectations lead to the most effective instructional practices.

What about grade-level distinctions in standards?

Although the Common Core State Standards are organized by grade level, it is important to remember that whether you are teaching kindergarten, first grade, or second grade, student expertise will encompass a similar range of abilities. There will be kindergartners who read the same texts enjoyed by second graders and there will be second graders who are early emergent readers. It is also important to recognize that learning to read and write does not follow a linear path. Learning occurs recursively within and across grade levels. Effective instruction provides students with multiple opportunities to revisit concepts and enact their learning over time with increasing difficulty. It is important for teachers to look at expectations horizontally (within grade levels) and vertically (from one grade level to the next), recognizing that each classroom is filled with unique individuals who encompass a range of knowledge and abilities. So, once again, while the standards detail grade-specific expectations, the real decisions about how and when students should demonstrate standard-specific learning are left to teachers' judgment.

Conclusion: Demystified Yet?

Demystifying means making the strange familiar or at least less intimidating. In this case, we hope to have communicated that demystifying also means chasing down directives to determine whether they are myth or reality. When directives contradict what you know to be true about good teaching, they need to be addressed. So, demystifying the Common Core State Standards has much to do with reading the fine print, interpreting it by using sound knowledge of theory and practice, and then taking action to enable teaching in ways that will benefit your students the most.

Demystifying also has to do with recognizing the good work that you already do. Take a moment and list everything you hope for your students in an academic year: skills, dispositions, proficiencies, motivations, abilities. It is likely that your list encompasses the content of every standard in any set of educational guidelines required by your state or district, plus much more. So, as you consider standards, begin by trusting your best teaching. As Katie Wood Ray (2006) writes, "there is no challenge to try and somehow infuse [teaching] with high standards; if you're [teaching] good stuff, high standards are already there" (p. 185).

Hand-in-hand with valuing what you already do well, demystifying also occurs through teachers' engagement in ongoing professional study. The knowledge we acquire as professional educators allows us to address standards with wisdom. With knowledge, we need not be constrained by standards. We can plan and teach with confidence and tenacity. In the following section, we glimpse into preK and primary grades classrooms as nine tenacious teachers share ways that they use their knowledge to meet the needs of their students. They invite us into teaching/learning moments and share ways that they focus on children, create culturally and linguistically responsive curricula, and meet standards by teaching in "warm-demanding" ways (Gay, 2011, p. 57).

II

Teachers and Students in Classrooms

⊚ Introduction

Every teacher loves to be the fly on the wall in the classrooms of other teachers. We stop by a neighbor's room and notice the vibrancy of students' latest pieces of writing. We scan the room and observe children and teachers encouraging, celebrating, teaching, and learning. We come away with renewed energy to transform our own learning communities. The teachers featured in this section invite readers into their classrooms in much the same way—to experience teaching in a time of standards that begins with the child and builds on the foundational principles introduced in Section I. In Section III of this book, questions are provided to prompt reflection and discussion about your own classrooms using these vignettes as jumping-off points.

At the core of their teaching, these educators are committed to creating "exciting places for exploration and growth" (http://www.saveourschoolsmarch.org/2011/05/02/heres-to-the-teachers). They believe strongly that equitable practices should draw on more than one cultural model of learning. For example, they are dedicated to helping students maintain home languages while adding proficiencies in Academic English. In Freida Hammett's classroom, for example, Korean, Hindi, and Mandarin are cherished along with the English that is foundational to instruction. Nancy Boggs, Mariel Laureno, Julia López-Robertson, and Jessica Keith bring students' Spanish language expertise into the curriculum as important resources. Tammy Freirson joins her preschoolers in the regular study of Spanish and she learns alongside the children as a parent introduces Hebrew. Carmen Tisdale is at the beginning of her exploration of using contrastive analysis to help students gain insight into the legitimacies and differences between African American Language and Academic English.

You will also see how these teachers create spaces for students to develop as critical consumers and producers of literacies. Mary Cowhey describes her second graders' involvement in the study of labor issues in the clothing industry. Janice Baines and Carmen Tisdale write about their first graders' collection of oral histories to preserve the stories of the historic African American community in which they live. Julia López-Robertson's second graders and their families explore issues of immigration through bilingual literature discussions.

Each teacher's section is written in three parts: (a) Meet the Teacher, (b) Teaching and Learning Moments, and (c) The Teacher's Journey: Pathways to Enacting Practices. Vignettes are organized by grade level. Following each set of grade-level vignettes, practices are charted to highlight teaching/learning moments as they connect to NCTE principles and beliefs and to specific Common Core State Standards. This is done to demonstrate that meeting standards can look quite different from one classroom to another and that when curriculum and teaching strategies are tailored to children's interests, cultural knowledge, language, and academic needs, standards fall easily into place.

So we welcome you into the classrooms of teachers who, like you, care deeply about children and their families, face challenges as well as successes every day, and continuously study the art and science of the profession in the pursuit of effective teaching for all children. While effort has been made to include a geographically, culturally, and linguistically diverse range of classrooms, this collection of classrooms is obviously not comprehensive. For that reason, we urge you to read with an eye to possibilities for your own classroom no matter the grade level or demographic. Use these stories as jumping-off points for reflection about developing "alternative visions for what is worth cherishing in public schools" (Nieto, 2003, p. 8) in a time of Common Core State Standards or anytime.

Reading and Writing in Preschool and Kindergarten

2

◎ "The word on the street is that Olivia read a book today!" Preschoolers Learning Languages and Literacies

by Susi Long with Tammy Frierson

Meet the Teacher

Tammy Frierson teaches in a bright and busy classroom of twenty-three four- and five-year-olds. Tammy is the lead teacher, but she will be the first to tell you that her teaching assistant, Mrs. Robinson, and the school's Spanish teacher, Sra. Herron, are critical to the classroom's success. Mrs. Robinson has been at the school for thirty-two years, has taught the parents of some of the students, and is greatly admired for her wisdom in all things early childhood. Sra. Herron comes several days a week to share her enthusiasm for and knowledge of Spanish language and heritage with the children. Tammy's admiration of her teaching partners is the first thing readers should know about her. This is who Tammy is—a teacher with tremendous expertise who values those who bring further wisdom and perspective to her classroom.

Tammy has been teaching for fourteen years, eleven of those in this child development program serving a suburban public school system in the southeastern United States. The program was provided by the district as a service to the community and, although tuition-based, many of the children attend with the support of state-funded vouchers and grants for low-income families.

In Tammy's classroom, eight of the children are African American, eight are European American, one is Latino, and one is biracial (Black/Latino). Seventeen of the students identify as Christians, one is Jewish, one is Muslim, and one is Hindu.

Tammy views this diversity as a blessing and, with the help of family members, she ensures that the class celebrates Ramadan, Chanukah, Christmas, Diwali, and Kwanzaa. Honoring each child and his or her family is basic to Tammy's ability to build a community that, as she says, is truly a family.

Teaching and Learning Moments in Tammy's Classroom

Wisdom, calm, and *joy* are words that come to mind after sitting for only a few minutes in Tammy's classroom. As we slip into one of the tiny chairs at a table full of puzzle pieces and books, we see all of the children seated in a large oval on the gathering carpet. Four-year-old Nate's mother has already joined the class this morning and is sharing their family's Chanukah traditions. She teaches songs and shares language, adding the lyrics and some Hebrew characters to the English and Spanish words already on the whiteboard. Tammy joins the lesson by asking carefully posed questions and making strategic comments to help the children get as much as possible out of the experience. Tammy's sensitivity to the needs of the children and to celebrating Nate is apparent as, at various points in the conversation, she naturally interjects with comments and questions such as:

"So tonight at Nate's house, what are they going to do?"

"Did you know that Menorah means 'light'? It has nine lights. One needs to be higher than the others."

"Is there a light in the Temple that burns constantly?"

"I have another question: What in the world is a *latke*?"

[Speaking to Nate's mother] "I'm so happy you came. Oh my goodness, I'm overwhelmed with all that I learned."

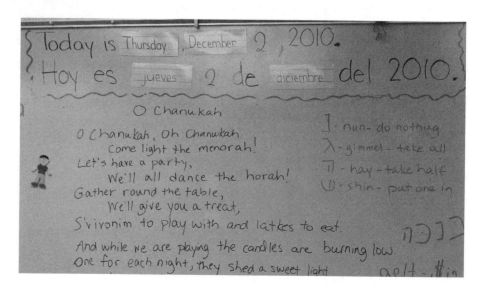

As Nate's mother leaves, Tammy announces to the children, "Olivia came in with a book today. I feel that it is important for her to do what?"

"Read it!" the children call out.

"Olivia, you've been working on this book?"

Olivia nods.

"Well, bless your heart. Let's give Olivia our undivided attention." Olivia settles onto the bench at the front of the room. She opens her book and begins to read aloud, showing the pages to the class as she has

seen Tammy do many times before. The class listens with rapt attention. Tammy sits close by so that, now and then, in an ever-so-gentle voice, she can support Olivia's reading of the text. This is clearly a landmark day for Olivia. As she finishes the book, Tammy announces, "The word on the street is that Olivia read a book today! Mrs. Robinson, will you tell anyone you see that Olivia read a book today?" Mrs. Robinson responds, "You know I will."

The children have been sitting for quite a while so Tammy stands up and tells them, "Now we're going to exercise. You stand up too. Okay, the inside of me is going to breathe in and out. Now I'm going to wake up my toes. Inside my shoes, my toes are moving. My knees are rocking. My bottom's swinging. My shoulders

are moving. My neck is swinging. My head is bopping. Let's do it and count to twenty. One, two, three, four." The children move with her, captured by her voice, the language of her direction, and her easy guidance of their movements.

As they exercise, Sra. Herron, the Center's Spanish teacher, quietly enters the room and joins in their movements. After the children sit down, she begins her Spanish lesson. Tammy sits in a chair just behind the children so that she can participate as a learner, but also to help focus students' attention and responses through her participation. The interplay between Tammy and Sra. Herron is elegant and seamless. They finish each other's sentences in

ways that clarify information and extend learning. As Sra. Herron begins to call roll, Tammy calls out, "¡Presente!", modeling the correct response for the children. When Sra. asks the children, "¿Cómo estás?", Tammy answers with great enthusiasm, "¡Bueno!", and the children repeat, "¡Bueno!"

Then Sra. Herron leads the children in singing a "Buenos Dias" song. Tammy and Mrs. Robinson join in, again supporting the children in participating and learning. They do the same thing when Sra. reads a book to the children in Spanish. At one point, Sra. comes to a passage about a flashlight. She explains that she keeps one on her bedside table. She asks Tammy if she has a flashlight on her bedside table. Tammy answers, "Sí," and then models how learning language sometimes means taking the initiative to ask for help: "And so how do I say "bedside table" in Spanish?"

"Mesita."

"Oh, mesita. I can say mesita," Tammy announces proudly.

This creates a space for Sra. to provide another language lesson: "Remember boys and girls, we say ita when we mean that something is very little. Table is mesa so little table is mesita." Then she asks about a favorite cartoon character. "Does Dora have a flashlight?"

One of the children answers, "Yes. Do you want to know what color it is? Roja."

"¡Bueno!" says Sra. and Tammy applauds. Then Sra. asks, "Is it grande or pequeña?"

"It is pequeña," answers one of the children.

"Yo linterna roja," chimes in another child intending to say, "I have a red flashlight."

Sra. congratulates him for his approximation: "See, he is trying to put all of his words in Spanish together. Good job!" Then Mrs. Robinson extends the learning further by asking, "I want to know—do we have a linterna at school?"

"¡Sí!" the children shout.

When Sra. asks, "¿Donde?", Mrs. Robinson goes to a cabinet and comes back with the class flashlight. "Is it grande or pequeña?" The children reply, "¡Pequeña!" Sra. asks why they have a flashlight in the school and the children offer two answers: "To look in our throats if we're sick" and "Because one time, I had to get a bead out of my ear."

"We're not going to have that anymore!" says Tammy.

"¡No más!" agrees Sra.

"¡No más!" agree the children.

In unplanned yet natural ways born of shared goals for and commitment to the children's learning, language is developed and used as the children experience Hebrew, Spanish, and English, all in the course of one early morning gathering time. The Spanish lesson finishes with a song and Tammy congratulates the children: "You know what? Today I was so proud of you all. You all have been so patient! So today I'm extremely . . . "

"Happy!" calls out one of the girls, and Tammy replies, "Girl, I'm always happy. But today I'm a little more than happy. I'm feeling generous. Do you know what *generous* means? It means that you give more than usual." Tammy shares her generosity by directing the children to centers around the room. She suggests that Nate show Sam how to play the dreidel game he brought to school so that Sam can teach other children.

Mary, Corrine, and Logan head to a writing table to work on books they are making. Mrs. Robinson moves to the table where she will read and write with a group of the youngest children. A calm hum of activity permeates the classroom as children build with blocks, make alphabet books, write in journals, cut, draw, count, organize, and create.

Tammy sits down to hear Nate and Samuel read and then guides them to illustrate and write about the story. Another child brings her writing to share. "Look at that!" Tammy exclaims in genuine pleasure at the girl's accomplishment. Tammy crosses the room to work with a group of children learning to tell time. On the way, she notices one little boy pulling his rug over to work quietly by a classroom visitor. "He enjoys being right there beside you while he's working," she says, her

sensitive knowledge of the children revealed once again. Then Tammy sits down on the floor with her group, holds up a large cardboard clock, and begins her lesson. And the room continues to hum.

Tammy's Journey: Pathways to Enacting These Practices

Tammy's teaching convictions and classroom practices have grown over the years from her feelings about children and their families. As she says, "Parents leave their children with me every day. You have to be real and sincere about your relationships with them. I don't think about making an effort to embrace families from diverse backgrounds in my classroom. It's what we do."

Tammy loves teaching in a family-grouped setting. She first meets the children when they are three years old and continues to teach them for three years. Tammy says, "In the first year, I'm just getting to know a part of their personalities. In the second year, they are really finding their place in the classroom, and by the third year, they know me very well—my humor, my style, my expectations—and then they can help the younger children by modeling their responses to me." Tammy doesn't see teaching a multiage class as more stressful than teaching any other class. She recognizes that even a class of all four-year-olds or a class of five-year-olds would encompass a span of abilities, experiences, and understandings similar to those of her group of three- to five-year-olds.

In terms of standards and other guidelines, Tammy appreciates that her administrator listens—genuinely listens—when she and other teachers question suggested modes of teaching. She feels fortunate that her administrator respects and "chooses to trust" the decisions she makes and engages with teachers in collaborative professional study. Tammy does not take for granted that her administrator honors teachers' autonomy as well as their commitment to continued professional growth. As Tammy says, "It's nice to know that you can say 'no' and it's not a power struggle."

Tammy is deeply committed to career-long professional learning. Currently, she is studying culturally relevant practices with a faculty study group, taking classes to gain Montessori certification, and studying new languages alongside her students. These are commitments that keep her going as a professional and that have supported her through the years. She perseveres in professional study because she worries about "all of the programs that are often imposed on teachers by people who have no idea about classrooms" and believes that teachers need to continue to build their professional knowledge so they can get involved and make decisions for their own schools and classrooms.

⊚ Listening as Key to Supporting Kindergarten Writers

by Katie Van Sluys with Mariel Laureano

Meet the Teacher

In her ninth year of teaching, Mariel Laureano became a kindergarten teacher at the same Chicago public school where she began her teaching career. The school is situated within a small community that has historically been home to predominately Latino/a families. Mariel has worked with students and families in the community through many of the challenges that accompany the gentrification of neighborhoods, including the displacement of families and threats of school closings. Before teaching kindergarten, Mariel worked for seven years as a middle grades teacher and for one year as a school-based literacy coach. One of Mariel's great qualities as a literacy coach and a classroom teacher is that she is, first and foremost, a listener. From the youngest child to her learning colleagues, Mariel listens. Through careful listening, she is able to provide necessary support for learners as they inquire into issues, concepts, and ideas that matter.

In the following vignette, we enter Mariel's classroom as her kindergartners begin their day. Through the events of one morning, we see ways that Mariel lives her belief that careful listening is foundational to good teaching, as well as ways that she builds on the resources children bring to school, including home languages. She views such resources as assets to be celebrated and developed throughout students' lives.

Teaching and Learning Moments in Mariel's Classroom

Walking into Mariel's kindergarten classroom, children, family members, colleagues, and visitors are immediately aware that this environment is not only physically inviting but is also a space filled with energy. Visitors are compelled to linger, watch, listen, and attend to the many ways that class members learn *and* teach as they read, write, draw, move, talk, sing, and so on. One of the first things visitors see is a small table set up with a simple notebook housing children's daily sign-in lists. Turning the pages, we see children's writing progress from copying their first names to the independent use of conventions as they write their first and last names using spacing and uppercase as well as lowercase letters.

Looking up from the notebook, we notice that the walls of the classroom are lined with student work and tools for student learning. For example, we see an interactive

An alternative option to the interactive word wall is to have students keep word journals; set aside specific times each day to add to them. Students could be encouraged to trade words with classmates to expand their knowledge.

Children can help select books for baskets, making decisions about genre, topics, and stories that would be purposeful and appealing. Twenty minutes could be set aside on Fridays for students to fill book baskets for the next week.

word wall placed at a level where five- and six-year-olds can remove the words to use them in support of their reading and writing and return them when finished. Adjacent to the word wall, a colorful rug designates a class meeting space partitioned off by a bookcase on one side and kindergarten-size benches on the other side.

Books are arranged in baskets in the classroom library so that book covers always face outward with clear labels separating books by topic, genre, and language, for example, "Animal Books" and *"Libros en Español."* Additional book baskets are placed in the center of each round table in the classroom. The baskets are filled with a wide range of books to represent different student interests, reading abilities, and classroom themes of inquiry. Today, for example, a basket at Javier's table speaks to his current curiosity about nocturnal animals. It contains books about bats as well as a variety of other nonfiction books with diverse text features and organization. A basket at Itzel's table contains nonfiction books as well as storybooks such as *Green Eggs and Ham* in both Spanish and English.

The cozy, purposeful feeling in this room is deepened by features such as the fish tank, the daily letter written by the teacher to the children (posted for everyone to read), and student work hung from the clotheslines strung across the room. Each day in this classroom is unique and characterized by a lively hum of people engaged in serious, important work, but each day is also grounded in predictable structures that give children support and confidence.

To understand more about a few of these predictable structures, we spend time in Room 106 on a particular morning to follow the children as writers and readers. As usual, the children enter the room to find their morning work waiting for them. Today, they are asked to make connections to a fish diagram that fascinated them during whole-class shared reading the previous day. Building

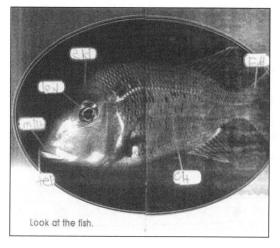

Look at the fish.

from their interest, Mariel has photocopied the diagram, deleting the words labeling the head, tail, scales, fin, and so on. The children check the front board and see that as their first task of the day, they are invited to label their fish diagrams and then make a diagram of their own. After hanging up backpacks and signing in, the children settle into their labeling tasks, excited to pick up where they left off the day before. While the children work, Mariel attends to the typical morning needs of individual children and then begins conferring with students about their writing.

As she kneels by Tomás, he points to the fish's scales on the diagram and asks, "What is this?"

"What do *you* think?" Mariel replies, turning the responsibility back to the child. "Skin," Tomás responds, and he begins to subvocalize sounds as he works to construct the word *skin* to label the scales on his diagram: "/s/ /k/ /i/." Knowing the child's needs at this moment in time, Mariel makes the decision not to correct his word choice (*skin* instead of *scales*), but to focus on supporting completing his construction of the word *skin* by helping him think about the ending sound. "What else do you hear in *skin*?" she asks. "Say the word out loud and think about the very last sound you hear."

A labeling exercise could work with almost any topic of inquiry and presents a great way to build from prior knowledge and vocabulary.

Mariel leaves Tomás and makes her way around the class as children draw support from her but also from each other and from the resources around the room. Some children walk over to a class-made diagram posted on the wall to gain further insights about which parts of a diagram are considered labels. Others talk quietly with each other as they make decisions about what should be written on the labels and how to construct words.

Productive talk of this kind does not emerge in a vacuum. Mariel consistently provides whole-group, small-group, and one-to-one demonstrations of how to think about constructing texts. She is explicit in asking the children to think in the same way when they work alone or with classmates. She frequently validates this kind of thinking by celebrating specific instances of its occurrence: "Did you see the way Tomás was thinking about how to write *skin* today? Tomás, would you please tell us what you did?"

As morning work time comes to a close, Mariel uses the beginning and ending sounds of children's names as a signal for them to gather their work and transition to morning meeting: "If your name starts with /z/, bring your work. If your name ends in /n/, bring your work." During group meeting, Mariel takes the opportunity to build on the students' enthusiasm for yesterday's nonfiction book about fish to deepen their ability to use and create informational texts. Today she introduces a new book, Steve Jenkins's *What Do You Do with a Tail Like This?* Briefly, she guides the children to make predictions about the text as they explore the cover and title. The children share their curiosities about the book, and Mariel reads a few selected pages aloud, pages that attend to what various animals do with their ears. She stops now and then to discuss new insights about content, but also about ways the author presents information using both text and illustration. Then she suggests that the class also create a book about ears—about what animals do with their ears—and each child will create a page.

Student-made pages for class books can be about any topic of study and are easy to put together. Hint: Take digital photos of children's illustrations and writing and download into PowerPoint to make pages of books that can be projected and/or printed and bound.

Javier heads to his seat, eager to share facts and findings from his active, science-oriented reading life, which includes many books about bats. As a writer who has spent much of his first five years of life thinking and learning in Spanish, Javier's oral language skills in English reveal his experience as an emerging bilingual speaker. Sensitive to this, Mariel is deliberate in supporting his use of Spanish while providing well-planned opportunities for him to continue adding English to his language repertoire. Javier begins by drawing a bat on the top of his paper. Mariel approaches him for a brief conference:

MARIEL: OK, you've got your bat, what do you want to say about the bat?

JAVIER: He's creepy because he can use his ears. When some things talk, he flies and follows the noise where it's coming from.

MARIEL: So the bat uses his ears to follow the noise.

JAVIER: [Javier begins to write: *A bat is cool because he uses his*—Then he makes the sounds out loud as he attempts to write *ears*] h . . . e . . . e . . . r . . . s

MARIEL: Let's stop and review to see what you can add to it. [She reads] A bat is cool because he uses his ears [pause]. What did you say he uses his ears for?

JAVIER: Following the noise.

One-on-one conferences provide unparalleled opportunities to gauge an individual child's learning. Fit in conferences at every opportunity—as children are coming in, when they are at centers, on the playground, anywhere!

Mariel's teaching strategy is clear: She asks a strategic question and then she listens. While listening, she focuses on understanding what Javier wants the reader to know. Javier regularly uses talk to frame and refine his thinking—he talks as he writes. Mariel knows it is important for him to use spoken English and, at times, Spanish to try out his thinking, to express what he knows. Then she uses her talk to reframe his thinking in conventional English by repeating his ideas back to him in somewhat different form. She echoes his thinking so he can hear new possibilities for expressing his ideas. She helps Javier understand that his message is what matters most, but that it is also important to use certain conventions to be able to communicate his message clearly to others.

Through this moment of teaching and learning, Mariel learns a little bit more about what Javier knows and needs to know as he continues to develop as a code breaker, meaning maker, and text user. She sees that he is beginning to differentiate between fiction and nonfiction, can identify and use text features to tell more about the subject at hand, and hear sounds in words as he segments sounds for writing. Through this moment, she learns that Javier knows that writers write for readers and that one's reading life can directly influence one's writing life.

Mariel's Journey: Pathways to Enacting These Practices

It is clear from this glimpse into Mariel's classroom that conferencing is a cornerstone of her teaching as she aims to meet individual student needs. She entered the profession with a commitment to making a place for talk as foundational to writing, but she deepened that commitment through her involvement in ongoing professional study. Over the years, she has continued to perfect her ability to engage the children in one-to-one conferences as well as whole-class discussions and then to listen, learn from their talk, and tailor her teaching to match their needs and potentials. She is able to do this by thinking about each child in conjunction with her strong professional knowledge about literacy learning and teaching and with her knowledge of each child's family and community resources.

Mariel came to this commitment to listening because of her professional reading, but also because of her convictions about knowing the children well. Her teaching is guided by a strong sense of responsibility to child, family, and community. She sees school as a community space that requires full inclusion and participation of families and community members, but she recognizes that she must take responsibility for engaging them by making herself a part of local community issues and getting to know families and their out-of-school lives. She believes that fulfilling her commitment to the community also means taking responsibility for moving each child forward in specific ways by listening to build on what the child already knows and then presenting new information to ensure growth.

Charting the Practice in Prekindergarten and Kindergarten

Have a look at a few of the teaching/learning moments in Tammy's and Mariel's classrooms as they address principles that NCTE has identified as foundational to great teaching and as they meet specific Common Core State Standards.

NCTE Principles and Beliefs Enacted in These Moments	Teaching/Learning Moments in Tammy's Class	Teaching/Learning Moments in Mariel's Class
Home cultures and languages are celebrated and used as foundational to instruction. *Students develop an understanding of and respect for diversity in language use, patterns, and dialects across cultures, ethnic groups, geographic regions, and social roles.*	Nate's mother teaches a Chanukah song, Hebrew language, and religious traditions. Tammy reinforces by asking questions and reminding the children of Nate's lighting of the Menorah. Sra. Herron reads aloud from a Spanish picture book and teaches a Spanish song. Tammy and Mrs. Robinson join in as learners. Tammy asks Nate to teach the dreidel game to Samuel who will, in turn, teach it to other children.	In a 1–1 conference, Mariel helps Javier make connections between his home language and his acquisition of English. The classroom library includes children's books in both English and Spanish. Book baskets are organized by topic, genre, and language. The basket for books in Spanish is labeled *Libros en Español*.
Key to high-quality formative assessment is teachers making time and space to listen to and interact with individual students as they work. *Teachers who know how to listen and what to listen for can inform instruction immediately as well as for the long-term.*	Tammy invites Olivia to read to the class and celebrates. Because she knows Olivia well as a reader, she recognizes that this is a critical point in her learning. Tammy listens to Nate and Samuel read and then guides them to write a story based on their reading.	As Mariel conferences 1–1, she listens to determine which instructional moves to take next. She can respond, question, and teach because she knows each child well. Mariel teaches Tomás through their conference, then uses his example to teach a spelling strategy to the class: "Did you see the way Tomás was thinking about how to write *skin* today? Tomás, would you please tell us what you did?"
Using anchor texts—the work of other authors—as the foundation for teaching writing, for learning through the demonstrations of others, is essential whether learning to write fiction or nonfiction texts. *Children learn vocabulary, word patterns, letter-sound correspondences, and other skills best when they are supported in doing so explicitly, yet in the context of meaningful oral and print experiences.*	Children experiment with writing and reading at centers including collaborating on creating a book. Sra. Herron uses a Spanish language read-aloud as a jumping-off point for teaching the diminutive of the word, *mesa—mesita*. Tammy highlights new vocabulary in the context of giving directions to the class, for example, using and defining the word *generous*.	Mariel builds from students' enthusiasm about a nonfiction book she has read aloud to support them in learning to label their own diagrams. Mariel uses the book *What Do You Do with a Tail Like This?* to provide a model for nonfiction writing. As she reads aloud, she points out writing decisions made by the author. Mariel offers regular demonstrations of writing through her daily letters to the class. Mariel uses sounds in students' names as a way of transitioning the class and reinforcing phonemic awareness.

Where do you see these Common Core State Standards for kindergarten supported in Tammy's and Mariel's practices?

Language

- Standard L.K.1. Demonstrate command of the conventions of standard English grammar and usage when writing or speaking.
  - Print many upper- and lowercase letters.
  - Use frequently occurring nouns and verbs.
  - Form regular plural nouns orally by adding /s/ or /es/ (e.g., dog, dogs; wish, wishes).
  - Understand and use question words (interrogatives) (e.g., who, what, where, when, why, how).
  - Use the most frequently occurring prepositions (e.g., to, from, in, out, on, off, for, of, by, with).
  - Produce and expand complete sentences in shared language activities.

- Standard L.K.4. Determine or clarify the meaning of unknown and multiple-meaning words and phrases based on kindergarten reading and content.
  - Identify new meanings for familiar words and apply them accurately (e.g., knowing *duck* is a bird and learning the verb *to duck*).
  - Use the most frequently occurring inflections and affixes (e.g., -ed, -s, re-, un-, pre-, -ful, -less) as a clue to the meaning of an unknown word

Reading: Literature

- Standard RL.K.2. With prompting and support, retell familiar stories, including key details.
- Standard RL.K.4. Recognize common types of texts (e.g., storybooks, poems).

Reading: Foundational Skills

- Standard RF.K.1. Demonstrate understanding of the organization and basic features of print.
  - Follow words from left to right, top to bottom, and page-by-page.
  - Recognize that spoken words are represented in written language by specific sequences of letters.
  - Understand that words are separated by spaces in print.
  - Recognize and name all upper- and lowercase letters of the alphabet.

Writing

- Standard W.K.2. Use a combination of drawing, dictating, and writing to compose informative/explanatory texts in which they name what they are writing about and supply some information about the topic.

Speaking and Listening

- Standard SL.K.1. Participate in collaborative conversations with diverse partners about kindergarten topics and texts with peers and adults in small and larger groups.
  - Follow agreed-upon rules for discussions (e.g., listening to others and taking turns speaking about the topics and texts under discussion).
  - Continue a conversation through multiple exchanges.

- Standard SL.K.2. Confirm understanding of a text read aloud or information presented orally or through other media by asking and answering questions about key details and requesting clarification if something is not understood.

3 Culturally Relevant Literacy Practices in Three First Grades

◎ Reading Instruction through Music, Oral History, and Hand Jive

by Janice Baines and Carmen Tisdale

Meet the Teachers

We are first-grade teachers—teammates who teach down the hall from each other in an urban elementary school in the southeast. Each of the students in our classrooms is African American. The school is situated within an African American community listed on the National Register of Historic Places; however, the community's rich history of Black artisans, professionals, and social reformers is too often masked by media stereotypes that focus more on gang presence, crime, unemployment, and our school's poverty index, which is 99.19 percent. In the past decade, the community has also faced issues of gentrification, resulting in the displacement of members of a once close-knit community.

We both participate in a professional study group through which we explore culturally relevant pedagogies. After our first year of study, we named our group Teachers for Equity in Education (TEE) because of the focus of our work. We read professional literature, learn from visiting experts, attend conferences, and try out new ideas in our classrooms. We invite you into our classrooms to witness some of those ideas in practice as first graders learn literacy through music, hand jive, oral history, and other culturally responsive practices.

Teaching and Learning Moments in Janice's Classroom

Walking down the primary wing of our school's hallway, visitors arrive at room P39, the home of my Brave Bears: six- and seven-year-olds who are a gift to the community, to the school, and to me. The voices of young learners capture my heart every day just as they capture the hearts of visitors who spend time with us. Within the walls of our classroom lives a family of learners—tomorrow's promise.

Glancing around the room, your eyes will be drawn to the words of an upbeat classroom rap written to set the tone for the year and to build reading instruction from students' home knowledge. The lyrics to "I Can Read Swag" (performed to the rhythm of a student favorite, Soulja Boy's "Pretty Boy Swag") are posted around the room and printed in multiple copies of spiral-bound books placed in book baskets, at listening centers, and at computers. The children read our "Swag" books independently and I use them for shared reading by projecting the pages of the book on our SMART Board. Using "Swag," I introduce, review, and solidify skills: directionality, one-to-one correspondence, high-frequency words, compound words, contractions, word patterns—"If you can read *swag* you can read *bag, tag, flag, wag*"—and much more. Those skills are reinforced as students work with the words and word patterns at "Swag" centers around the room. In whole-group, small-group, and one-to-one we also work to transfer "Swag" skills to trade books and leveled texts.

Through the song and the instruction that accompanies it, the children feel the strong message of the importance of reading. As they read the lyrics to "Swag," students recognize that they *are* readers. If you listen closely, you will hear the students whispering parts of the rap as they work at their tables and as they move around school.

We Are Family

By Ms. Baines' First Grade Class
September 2010

This is Ms. Myers. She grew up in the Waverly community. She told us so many important stories.

You will see them recognizing words from the rap in other contexts—in signs in the school hallway, in other books. Most important, "Swag" allows us to develop an unbreakable family bond. It is the song by which our class is known, a part of our shared history, our identity.

"I Can Read Swag" led to the development of other books that we use for instruction: *Meet Ms. Baines* and *We Are Family*. Again, multiple copies of the books can be found in book baskets, in centers, at the computer, and on the SMART Board screen as we read and learn with them.

P39 is also the home of the first books created by the students in the Preserving Waverly series. Students interviewed members of the historic community in which the school is situated and used videos of the interviews to support them in converting oral history to written text. The resulting books are also used for instruction and presented to the interviewees with great respect and gratitude.

Leaving P39, the children and their work will remain dear to your heart. From repetitive rap to personal narratives to interviews with community elders, every child will let you know that he or she *is* a reader.

Janice's Journey: Pathways to Enacting These Practices

As an undergraduate studying early childhood education, I learned about the importance of curriculum that reflects students' cultural backgrounds, and I tried several ways to incorporate it during my student teaching. Unfortunately, that curriculum was only a memory during my first two years as a first-grade teacher.

My school's achievement data was one of the first things that pierced this feeling for me. We were constantly at the bottom in all areas. I didn't like this and knew something had to change. I knew that my students must feel a sense of belonging and the love from me. But they also needed something more. I began taking classes and researching trends in early childhood education. Then I joined a small study group of teachers. The goal of the group has been to study and implement practices to support children through culturally relevant literacy methods.

An important aspect of my learning is recognizing that first graders come to school at different levels and that each child requires his or her own time frame and uniquely designed curriculum to develop those skills. I wanted to find ways to foster their learning and began to embrace the development of an environment that helps students see their potential and learn through the accomplishments and contributions of their people. So, every day, I listen to how students respond to class activities and reflect on their growth and my teaching methods to determine what might be transformed from traditional curriculum to more culturally relevant practices. I also look at interactions in the community and media representations of African Americans so I can be sure to use resources that promote positive images and contradict negative ones. I don't just use culturally relevant texts, but I infuse our discussions with information about history and heritage.

As I do this, I don't ignore the standards that our district requires. But, the thought of standards can be overwhelming. I used to say things such as, "We can't teach this standard unless students come with the previous standard mastered." So, I had to change my thinking. I now look at standards as one aspect of the "what" in understanding what children are supposed to learn. Culturally relevant pedagogy helps me broaden that "what" as I consider "how" to teach. For example, the standards don't say that children should learn to value their heritage and the heritage of others or that they should learn to code-switch across languages used in their communities and at school, but I know that is important. So, I've found that standards are easier to address when you don't look at them as the beginning and the end, but as one resource. To do that, I know that I have to continue studying my profession as well as trying and evaluating new ideas to build knowledge about educational theory and practices that support it.

Teaching and Learning Moments in Carmen's Classroom

As you walk into room P08, the first thing that stands out is the music playing. The students are welcomed each morning by jazz, old-school R&B, or hip-hop. Just one visit may have you doing the *Stanky Leg*, taught by the children, or singing along to "My Girl." But it isn't just the sound of music and the appeal of dance that sets us apart. This is just the beginning of students' learning through culturally relevant practices.

Our days begin with read-alouds that take us into the streets of Harlem where Ella Fitzgerald and Duke Ellington show us how it was "back in the day." We learn that Ragtime was music reflecting a period full of hope and survival. We travel through the low country of the Deep South to learn about the rich sounds of the Gullah language and its connections to our own African American Language. We study Black history through a rap written just for our class: "Black History Is Our History." We read books made by our student teachers about our community—the Waverly community.

> Historical figures often have profiles on the PBS website (http://www.pbs.org), many times with ideas for classroom instruction.

My name is Brian.
My favorite song is "Hit 'Em With That Flex."
I like it because it makes me sing.

Johnny Over the Ocean
Johnny over the ocean
Johnny under the sea
Johnny broke the mailbox
And blamed it on me
So I told ma
Ma told Pa
And Johnny got a spanking
Ha,ha,ha

Shared Reading is a time to celebrate our rich culture even more. Through a series of class-made books, the children experience literature that is relevant to their lives: *When I Was a Little Girl* (a book that I wrote to introduce myself during the first weeks of school), *My Name Is* (each child wrote a page to introduce themselves), books with favorite hand jives (*Miss Mary Mack*; *Johnny Over the Ocean*), *Music We Love* (about the children's favorite songs), and *My Girl* (page-by-page lyrics to *my* favorite childhood song). We also created books after the students collected oral histories by interviewing people from their community, the Waverly community. This allowed the children to honor their elders and their community and see new possibilities for their lives.

As I read aloud, the children follow along, reading each word as the pages are projected on the large screen in the front of the classroom. Because they relate to stories, the music, and the hand jives, there are cheers of excitement as the children see themselves in the books. At the same time, the books—filled with high-frequency words, new vocabulary, and material for teaching almost every literacy skill—form the basis for my literacy curriculum.

At least ten copies of each book have been printed and spiral-bound and are found throughout the room. You will find children at listening centers singing— sometimes rather loudly—as they read our book, *My Girl,* and learning one-to-one correspondence and directionality as they point to each word in the book. Moving along, you will see children engaged in word study using words and word patterns from class books. Another group wanders around the room, reading and doing the hand jives plastered on the walls. Other children are reading digital versions of the books at the computer center or they are snuggled into pockets throughout the room reading our books while listening to jazz playing in the background. Still others are meeting with me for conferences or small-group instruction using our class books to learn skills and how to transfer those skills to trade books and leveled texts. For homework, I send home take-home books (smaller versions of our books), along with assignments for families and children to read and work with words together.

But at the heart of all of this is music, as we focus on the sounds that have kept people going whether in Harlem, the Sea Islands of South Carolina, or in our own neighborhood. As a people, music has always been important. It permeates our lives at every turn. So, it is befitting that we also learn from it.

Carmen's Journey: Pathways to Enacting These Practices

I began this journey into the study of culturally relevant practices not knowing what to expect or how I would feel about it. There was definitely a strong interest because of how I feel about the value of one's culture, so I joined a wonderful study group that revived my soul for teaching. My participation in Teachers for Equity in Education brightened me in areas that I didn't realize had been dulled. These experiences are the springboard for critical conversations that make a real difference in my classroom.

One aspect of our study is learning about language. Being African American, I know and speak our unique language, but I hadn't thought enough about how to express to my children that it's a good thing to be bilingual. I can help them learn the art of translation—how and when to make the switch between African American Language and Standard American English as speakers, readers, and writers. Now I am beginning to incorporate the art of translation into the work that I do every day.

Hand-in-hand with the study of language is learning about the kinds of texts that support children learning literacy. Using culturally relevant texts (the books we make and other books that reflect the children's worlds) has been critical because few of the books provided for reading instruction (across a wide range of companies that produce leveled texts) reflect stories and characters relevant to my students.

I find that it is surprisingly simple to address standards and still teach so that the children can relate. Each week, I look at the culturally relevant lessons I have planned and align them with required elements of the district pacing guide. It isn't a forced effort if I am sure to think outside of the suggested pace and consider the individual needs of my students. This process allows me to include skills that are important for the children to learn but that might not be addressed by a particular experience that I've planned. For example, a required skill is to learn about the Table of Contents, so we began including a Table of Contents at the beginning of each of our class-made books.

I have also learned that it's important to make the skills and strategies I'm teaching visible. So, to reassure administrators and parents, and to provide documentation for myself, I add a few pages at the end of each class-made book with headings such as "District High-Frequency Words Found in This Book" or "Word Families in This Book" or "Challenging Words in This Book." In this way, I can assure anyone who comes into my classroom that we are addressing pacing guide indicators and district expectations.

For me, considering standards without this culturally relevant foundation would be a lifeless way to teach and would not address the needs of my students. My kids and I are having a ball doing what feels natural and they *are learning*. I see the fruits of our labor. We are doing what focused first graders do in our attempt to be "the tightest first grade at Carver-Lyon." The tightest first grade? Yes, I use music *and* African American Language to settle into a family way in my classroom as we learn literacy and honor cultural heritage together.

⊚ Los Girasoles/The Sunflowers: Stories from First-Grade Writers

by Katie Van Sluys with Jessica Keith

Meet the Teacher

Jessica Keith began her teaching career in first grade when she joined the staff of a new Chicago public school. The school welcomes 800+ preschool through eighth-grade students who live in a neighborhood where Spanish is an important household and community resource. While physically large, the school building is an inviting place where children and family members arrive each day and are welcomed by faculty and staff. Because of the economic demographics of the community, a universal breakfast is provided for all learners. Each day, Sra. Keith greets her students—*los girasoles (the sunflowers,* a name chosen to identify her class of first graders)—at the front door and they make their way to their second-floor classroom. From the moment they enter the room, this first-grade community is engaged in rigorous work that expects them to use and develop language and literacy skills in both Spanish and English.

Jessica's classroom is part of a transitional bilingual program built on the understanding that children ultimately become more proficient bilinguals if they have opportunities to develop literacy proficiencies first in their home languages. Jessica's first grade emphasizes reading and writing in the students' first languages and oral language and receptive language skills in English. In second grade, the students ease into doing much more work with written English text, and by the end of third grade, they take on English full-time while maintaining Spanish proficiency.

The stories in the following vignette come from Sra. Keith's first year of teaching and learning with *los girasoles*. The glimpse into moments in Sra. Keith's work with six-year-old Diego and his classmate Juana provide powerful demonstrations of ways that sensitively planned lessons and strategically posed questions support the children as writers.

Teaching and Learning Moments in Jessica's Classroom

From the moment they enter the room, the children in Jessica's class are immersed in a print-rich environment with labeled book baskets, charts of student jobs, class data graphs, a growing word wall, morning messages, teacher-modeled writing, and student work. Children walk into the classroom and go right to work: They put away their things, get out their notebooks, work on morning math, and set up for breakfast. Sra. Keith uses her computer and projection board to write and display morning directions for students. On the big screen at the front of the room, the students can see instructions infused with digital photos and text in Spanish:

Text as it appeared on screen	English translation
Pon tu carpeta en la mesa.	*Put your folder on the table.*
Haz matemáticas de la mañana.	*Do your morning math.*
Desayuna y pon tu basura en el cesto.	*Eat your breakfast and put trash in the trash can.*

After reading the daily directions and completing the morning math problem written on the whiteboard, the children sit at tables of four quietly conversing and eating their breakfast. Then they come together as a class for their regular morning meeting and they segue into writing workshop. Sra. Keith teaches a mini-lesson to support the day's writing and sends the children to their tables to write while she makes her way around the room, stopping to conference with individual children in moments of focused instruction.

One day, following a whole-class lesson about how to write sequential instructions in nonfiction text, Diego decided to write about how to brush one's teeth. He shared his ideas passionately with the class and then raced to encode his ideas on paper. He began by writing a short string of letters: *Pnlap*. In conference, Sra. Keith

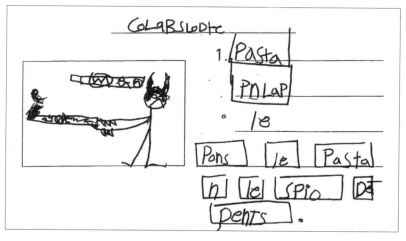

asked Diego, "Will you read what you have written?" and Diego said, "*Pone el pasta en el cepillo de dientes*" (Put the toothpaste on the toothbrush). Sra. Keith considered what she knew about Diego—that he could hear more sounds than were exhibited in *pnlap*. She knew this because she listened to Diego's subvocalization practices (whispering letter sounds) as he constructed text every day. So, she decided to use a particular teaching strategy to encourage him to access that knowledge. First, she asked Diego to count the number of words in the sentence he wanted to write. That was easy—there were eight words. Then she asked him to look at the writing on his paper—*Pnlap*—only one five-letter word. Diego immediately recognized the problem—he didn't have enough words to communicate his message! Sra. Keith drew eight little lines on his paper and asked Diego to repeat the sentence and to identify words that seemed bigger than the others. Together they made boxes on each line, bigger boxes for the bigger words, smaller boxes for the smaller words, and Diego filled in the boxes with letters for the sounds he heard. Lessons like this, taught

regularly, give Diego and his classmates the knowledge, confidence, and tools to become more proficient writers. Sra. Keith builds on these moments in large and small group as well as one-to-one.

In a second glimpse into Sra. Keith's classroom, several months later, we see the whole package—Sra. introduces an idea in a whole-group setting and then follows up as she conferences with individual children, in this case, Diego and his classmate, Juana. We enter the classroom as Sra. Keith introduces a sketch she has made of a *dinosaurio*. She demonstrates how the children might brainstorm to create characters as a way of beginning to write imaginative works of fiction. In her mini-lesson, she asks kids to first think about characters in a book read recently: *Miss Nelson Is Missing*. She asks the children, "*¿Cómo son los personajes?*" (What are the characters like?). The children chime in with "*mala*" (bad) referring to one character and "*simpatica*" (nice) and "*Les habla con un voz dulce*" (speaks with a sweet voice) describing another. Sra. Keith talks to them about how they can bring their own characters to life by using adjectives in the same way. The children practice by generating *adjetivos* to describe her *dinosaurio*: *grande* (big), *sucio* (dirty), *cariñoso* (loving), *perezoso* (lazy), and *los dientes sucios* (dirty teeth). With the list of adjectives complete, Sra. Keith facilitates a discussion about what this lazy dinosaur with dirty teeth might think or say—adding possible text options including "*¿Tengo un cepillo de dientes?*" (Can I have a toothbrush?) and "*¡No quiero dientes limpias!*" (I don't want clean teeth!). The children are instructed to develop their own characters, make lists of adjectives, and write some of the characters' thoughts or things their characters might say. The children go to work and conferences ensue. Sra. Keith stops by Juana's table to confer. She asks about Juana's character and Juana responds:

JUANA:	Mi personaje es un pingüino. Te gusta comer pescado.	*My character is a penguin. He likes to eat fish.*
SRA:	¿Cómo es el pingüino?	*Describe the penguin.*
JUANA:	Blanco.	*White.*
SRA:	¿Y qué más?	*And what else?*
JUANA:	Chiquito y cariñoso.	*Small and loving.*

Sra. Keith leaves Juana to continue writing. Juana uses the resources provided for her, consulting the word chart made with Sra. Keith to check her spelling of *cariñoso*.

At the same time, Diego is busy developing his character. Sra. Keith asks questions to push his writing:

SRA:	¿Quién es su personaje?	*Who is your character?*
DIEGO:	Es un superhero.	*He is a superhero.*
SRA:	¿Es Spiderman?	*Is he Spiderman?*
DIEGO:	No, es un goblin. Es malo. Está burlando.	*No, there is a goblin. He is bad. He is bullying/making fun of him.*
SRA:	¿Qué vas a escribir? ¿Qué son adjetivos para el goblin?	*What are you going to write? What are adjectives for the goblin?*
DIEGO:	Malo.... Verde....	*Bad . . . green*

Nearly two months after his nonfiction work about brushing teeth, Diego sets to work with similar energy and enthusiasm. This time, however, he is able to encode the adjectives to describe the *bad, green goblin* with much greater accuracy. Diego attends not only to listening to the sounds he hears, but he also takes the time to record more of them in his writing, a foundational skill in both Spanish and English.

These moments in Jessica's classroom capture her commitment to rigorous curricula that move learners beyond where they currently stand. In these brief moments, she taught them about verbally constructing text, then listening to sounds and encoding that thinking on paper. She also supported the children in developing characters and describing characters' actions by using adjectives while encouraging learners to use all the resources available to them including languages, literature, the classroom environment, and each other.

Jessica's Journey: Pathways to Enacting These Practices

Supporting the development of strong writers is one of Sra. Keith's goals. Early in this, her first year of teaching, she and her first-grade colleagues made the decision to support beginning writers by inviting them to write from their lives. Many of the students drew pictures. As the weeks went on, because of Sra. Keith's whole-class, small-group, and one-to-one instruction, many students began to add letters and write a few key word labels. Using her own writing, complete with illustrations and text, she actively narrates the decisions that writers make moment-to-moment as they commit print to paper. She confers with individuals and small groups of writers. In the beginning of the year, the students' texts were simple and short, but they allowed Sra. Keith to capture an image of what each student knew about writing and then tailor her teaching to build on and extend that knowledge.

While life in Sra. Keith's classroom is tailored to meet the needs of the learners in her care, her instructional decisions and students' growth also reflect/meet the expectations articulated in grade-level standards. *How* she uses and attends to the standards is what matters most. Standards, like any other resource, are among the tools that Sra. Keith uses to teach and support as, over time, *los girasoles* demonstrate their growth as writers. She, like other teachers in her building, plans for instruction based on her strong knowledge of (a) each child, (b) how children learn language, and (c) how people develop as readers and writers. With that knowledge, she can attend closely to what children are learning, modify her teaching accordingly, and address standards. In transitional bilingual programs, standards for Spanish language teaching are the recommended guidelines. As English language standards become a part of the students' school lives, Sra. Keith knows that it will be important to also maintain a focus on Spanish language standards if the children are to build bilingual proficiency.

Charting the Practice in First Grade

The following chart is provided so that educators can consider a few of the teaching/learning moments in Janice's, Carmen's, and Jessica's classrooms in terms of several NCTE principles as well as the Common Core State Standards.

NCTE Principles and Beliefs	Teaching/Learning Moments in Janice's Classroom	Teaching/Learning Moments in Carmen's Classroom	Teaching/Learning Moments in Jessica's Classroom
Home cultures and languages are celebrated and used as foundational to instruction. *Children read more on topics that interest them than on topics that are not of interest.* *Beginning readers learn words in the context of a story with familiar language better than they read words out of context.*	Janice created culturally relevant books and used them to teach high-frequency words, word patterns, and other conventions, as well as to motivate students and build their fluency. The books were used for independent reading, shared reading, small-group reading instruction, and 1–1 conferencing.	Carmen created culturally relevant books and used them to teach high-frequency words, word patterns, and other skills and to motivate students and build their fluency. The books were used for shared reading, independent reading, small-group instruction, and conferencing.	Jessica drew on Diego's Spanish to help him think through decisions about his writing. Children learned reading and writing vocabulary in the context of the daily instructions written in conjunction with familiar digital pictures.
Children learn about written language when more experienced writers provide demonstrations.			Jessica used the picture book (*Miss Nelson Is Missing*) to demonstrate what she expected the students to do as writers.
Students learn as they conduct research by generating ideas and questions and by posing problems. They gather, evaluate, and synthesize data from a variety of sources.	Students developed questions and interviewed community members to collect oral histories. They used taped interviews as the basis for developing nonfiction writing.		

Where do you see these Common Core State Standards supported in Janice's, Carmen's, and Jessica's vignettes?

Speaking and Listening

- Standard SL.1.1. Participate in collaborative conversations with diverse partners about grade 1 topics and texts with peers and adults in small and larger groups.
  - Follow agreed-upon rules for discussions (e.g., listening to others with care, speaking one at a time about the topics and texts under discussion).
  - Build on others' talk in conversations by responding to the comments of others through multiple exchanges.
  - Ask questions to clear up any confusion about the topics and texts under discussion.

- Standard SL.1.2. Ask and answer questions about key details in a text read aloud or information presented orally or through other media.

- Standard SL.1.3. Ask and answer questions about what a speaker says in order to gather additional information or clarify something that is not understood.

Reading: Foundational Skills

- Standard RF.1.2. Demonstrate understanding of spoken words, syllables, and sounds (phonemes).

- Standard RF.1.3. Know and apply grade-level phonics and word analysis skills in decoding words.

- Standard RF.1.4. Read with sufficient accuracy and fluency to support comprehension.

Reading: Literature

- Standard RL.1.4. Identify words and phrases in stories or poems that suggest feelings or appeal to the senses.

- Standard RL.1.10. With prompting and support, read prose and poetry of appropriate complexity for grade 1.

Reading: Informational Text

- Standard RI.1.3. Describe the connection between two individuals, events, ideas, or pieces of information in a text.

- Standard RI.1.10. With prompting and support, read informational texts appropriately complex for grade 1.

Poetry, Critical Literacies, and Literature Discussion in Second Grade

4

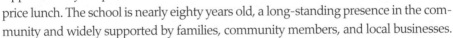 "Can I take pictures of my chickens?" Bringing Poetry to Life through Photography in a Second-Grade Writing Workshop

by Tasha Tropp Laman with Nancy Boggs

Meet the Teacher

Nancy Boggs is a second-grade teacher in an urban school located in the southeastern United States. There are approximately four hundred children in the school, drawing from local neighborhoods that include upper-middle-class homes and subsidized federal housing. There are more than fourteen languages represented in the school. Thirty-six percent of children are African American, 34 percent are White, 18 percent are Latino, 5 percent are Asian, 5 percent are multiracial, and less than 1 percent of students identify as Native American. Approximately 55 percent of children receive free or reduced-price lunch. The school is nearly eighty years old, a long-standing presence in the community and widely supported by families, community members, and local businesses.

Nancy began her teaching career twelve years ago. This is her eleventh year at this school and her sixth year teaching second grade. She grew up in a home where there was not much money and remembers what it felt like when teachers looked down on her family because of their financial circumstances. These experiences have clearly shaped her teaching. Nancy is committed to ensuring that children feel welcome in her classroom. Students who are new to English thrive there. Nancy views multiple languages as an asset. Even though she is a monolingual speaker of English, she is committed to learning words and phrases in languages spoken by her students and encourages the children to use their linguistic resources as tools for making meaning. She regularly invites parents who speak languages other than English into her class-room to teach her students about their languages and home countries.

In the following vignette, Nancy shares the latest work in her commitment to create culturally responsive practices through home, school, and community connections. In this case, she does so through poetry and photography.

Teaching and Learning Moments in Nancy's Classroom

Nancy's second-grade classroom is a lively space. An enormous carpet serves as a gathering space for morning meeting, read-aloud, shared reading, and writing mini-lessons. Nancy's rocking chair sits next to chart paper where she creates anchor charts for the children to refer to throughout the year. The students' desks are organized into small groups. There are books throughout the room organized according to topics, series, and authors.

Entering the classroom, we see students spread throughout the room: lying on the floor, standing at desks, and sitting in beanbag chairs. They are reading from a collection of photography and poetry books that Nancy has gathered to support the immersion phase in a poetry unit of study. She wants the students to read and hear lots of poetry before they begin to write their own. The students use sticky notes to record anything that they notice about the photos and poems in the books before them.

Gerardo, whose first language is Spanish, leans in closely and looks at Walter Dean Myers's poem, "Love that boy," featuring a photo by Samuel Roberts, and says, "¡Mira, una gallina!" (Look, a chicken!). Gerardo giggles at the photo of a serious-looking little boy with his arm around his chicken and places a sticky note on the page so that he can share it later.

Nancy calls the children to the rug and asks, "What did you notice about these poetry books?" The children's answers vary: "Some words rhyme and some don't." "There are long lines and short lines." "It can be about people or things." Geraldo holds up his book and shares, "This poem has a boy and a chicken!"

Nancy records students' comments on chart paper and, in a well-planned teaching moment, adds her own contributions as a way to introduce the students' next task. Nancy writes, "Sometimes poets write poems that go with photos that someone else has taken," and adds, "like Walter Dean Myers and Cynthia Rylant did." Then she writes, "Sometimes poets write poems about their own photos," and explains the new task to the class.

"Over the next week, you are going to take cameras home and take pictures of the people, places, and things that are close to your heart, and then you will write poems to go with your photos. You will only be able to take seven pictures, so you will have to think carefully about the pictures you take.

"Can I take pictures of my chickens?" Gerardo asks. "Can I take pictures of my chickens too?" Lyonel adds.

Nancy is thrilled: "Wow! I didn't know you had chickens! You are already thinking about your photos. Turn and tell your neighbor what you might photograph." The children begin talking about possible pictures of their families and communities, and as they share their ideas, Nancy records a list of possible photographs children could take in the coming days.

The next day, Nancy invites a parent who is a photographer to talk to the children about taking pictures. Ms. Smith shares photos she had taken, teaches the children how to take candid pictures, and emphasizes that they should take photos of people doing the things they normally do.

With disposable cameras purchased by university students who work with the children each week, the students begin taking photographs. A local shop gave Nancy and the other second-grade teachers a discount for developing film. Soon photographs begin to appear of parents playing guitar, family members cooking, grandparents reading, siblings sleeping, uncles playing computer games, pet dogs, cats, and, yes, chickens. With photographs in hand, Nancy is ready to begin conducting poetry lessons.

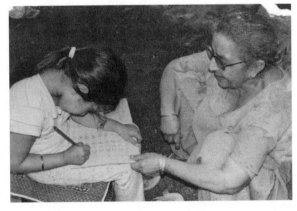

First, Nancy shares her own photographs and a poem that she has written to demonstrate how to use the photos to spark ideas for a poem and the difference between ordinary and poetic language. With the children seated in front of her, she explains how poets often write about everyday things in interesting ways.

"Think about how you can describe everyday things that your family does using poetic language. Like when your mom reads to you, it is like a soothing lullaby that puts you to sleep. Think about how much you love your family and what they mean to you. Here is poem that I wrote. Listen to how my poem brings these pictures together. . . . Does everyone see how I compared things like "My family is a shield because a shield protects?" and "a soothing bath would make me feel better when I am upset"?

> **Family**
> My mother sweet
>   Beloved chickpeas
>   Round as
>   The sun
>   Tastes like
>   A ball rolling
>   In my mouth
>   So good
> My family
>   Eating them
>   Just makes
>   My mouth water
> Seeing Dad working on his
>   Laptop smart
>   As a fox
> Family
>   Is a blanket
>   Of cotton
>   Cool and warm

> My mom is nice to me
> She makes me Spanish food
> I see her cooking on the stove
> She cooks and I smile
> My sisters make me happy
> When they sit and watch me
> With their dark cat eyes
>
> My dad works hard it
> Makes me happy when he comes with his t-shirt
> Stretching out like a tall oak tree
> Smelling like a new building he just built
>
> My chicks play and throw
> Their food with their long legs
> Like the vines and
> Scream like girls like they're mummies
> Trying to attack
> My family is nice to me.

> **My family**
> I love them all.
> My family makes me happy as the sun
> My family has eyes black as apple seeds
> My mom smells like peaches when she
> makes dinner
> My grandma speaks Chinese, I like to listen
> My family is special because they protect me
> from getting sick
> I love them all

Then Nancy makes a T-chart with the words *scientific language* and *poetic language* on either side of the T. She tells students to look out the classroom window and describe everyday things in scientific and poetic ways. Describing a tree, for example, instead of just saying the tree was tall, Maria says, "It's like a giant chocolate body with arms stretching out." Jason adds, "The branches are like a staircase for animals so they can get to their home." Lacey includes, "It's like wild hair." Luis offers, "It is an umbrella of shade."

Nancy explains to the children, "Today, when you write, look at your pictures and think about how you can use poetic language to describe them. Think about the words your family members say. Think about how these important people, places, and things make you feel." The children begin to write and soon the poetry behind their pictures comes to life.

The impact of this experience is evident in the children's completed poems. Three examples are provided here as representative of the rich and deeply thoughtful writing and the sophisticated use of vocabulary, turn of phrase, and metaphor that took place in Nancy's second-grade class. This occurred because she made a place to bring children's lives into her classroom, hand-in-hand with her well-planned and intentional teaching—supporting students' growth in the conventions and the craft of writing.

Nancy's Journey: Pathways to Enacting These Practices

It is clear that Nancy teaches in ways that bring the best of culturally relevant pedagogy into her classroom. It is also clear that she values the social nature of learning: she wants children to talk about what they are reading and writing. Over time, as she has tried these practices and paid attention to students' responses, she has come to see the power of her intentional teaching and the model she provides as students began to have productive peer conferences with each other. After much demonstration, instruction, practice, and feedback, her students now lean in and listen to each other read, and they share their most recent learning.

This does not happen, however, without intentionality and commitment to long-term professional study on Nancy's part. She is fortunate that her principal,

Dr. Baker-Parnell, encourages teachers to continually outgrow themselves and their current thinking. In the last five years, Nancy has participated in study groups facilitated by university faculty and attended workshops, and she reads extensively about teaching writing. During study group sessions, Nancy's involvement in conversations about equity and education and closing the achievement gap has deepened her knowledge about culturally relevant pedagogy, leading her to the photography/poetry experience and students' creation of rich and sophisticated texts.

Nancy finds that it is easy to incorporate the standards/indicators required by the district during Writing Workshop because the workshop structure and children's authentic writing allow her to meet so many of them. For example, standards require teaching students about figurative language and how to express their ideas in a variety of genres. The poetry and photo project incorporate those standards plus many more. The indicators for grammar require that the students use correct punctuation and noun-verb agreement, so she is sure to include something about each of these aspects in mini-lessons and conferences as the students work on their poetry.

Nancy sees the poetry/photography study as an opportunity for teaching the conventions of literacy, but also as a way to involve families and invite children's lives into the classroom. Families expressed how much they enjoyed the project and said their children taught *them* about poetry and photography. This sparked a new idea. Nancy envisions holding writing workshops with community members so that they can write their own poems. She sees this as an important way to support her multilingual students and their families: Poetry's brevity, repetition, and creative use of language create a genre where children can feel immediate success and are more open to revision. Families can witness how students' (and their own) levels of engagement and expertise increase as they create written texts of all kinds that grow out of *their* lives and interests.

⊚ Where's Your Shirt From?
Deepening Student Learning through Inquiry

by Mary Cowhey

Meet the Teacher

My name is Mary Cowhey. I teach in a small city in western Massachusetts. I have taught first and/or second grade for thirteen years, and I currently work as an ELL/Title I math teacher. The most diverse elementary school in the city, we have approximately 350 students. About 40 percent of them are students of color and 42 percent are eligible for free or reduced-price lunch. Most of the English language learners are native speakers of Spanish, with a smaller number who speak Urdu and other languages. I am the author of *Black Ants and Buddhists: Thinking Critically and Teaching Differently in the Primary Grades* and many articles and essays about teaching. I am committed to critical, authentic, integrated, culturally relevant teaching and building relationships with families and community to support student learning. The vignette below comes from a series of experiences that occurred in my second-grade classroom.

Teaching and Learning Moments in Mary's Classroom

Early in the school year, I distributed teddy bears to my second graders as a part of an emotionally responsive teaching initiative. One of the students asked if we could sew clothing for the bears. I'm not at all crafty, but I recruited a father to bring in his sewing machine and help make simple vests from felt rectangles. Students chose different colored felt, ribbons, and buttons and we made and trimmed vests for our bears.

Justin, a student who was excited about the sewing project, brought in a book called *How We Get Our Clothing* (1961) because it showed sewing machines, patterns, and clothing factories. It was full of stereotypes, but we did a critical reading of it. For example, I read aloud the caption under a photo of White women with beehive hairdos working at sewing machines: "This is where your clothing is made." I told the children that while this was true for me as a kid growing up in New York in the 1960s, it was mostly *untrue* for them now. Most of our clothing is manufactured in other countries. I explained that the workers in the photo looked like the mothers of my friends, many of whom worked in clothing factories in Brooklyn and belonged to the union, ILGWU.

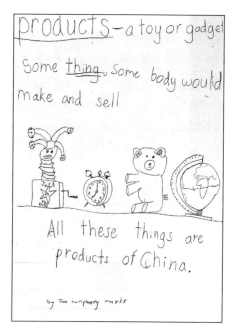

That reminded me of the "Look for the Union Label" song from the old television commercial. The students asked me to sing it; I have an awful singing voice, but since I still remembered most of the lyrics these thirty years later, I obliged. Justin asked, "Where do you look for the union label?" I'd scarcely said, "Well, labels are usually sewn into the back of your shirt or pants" when they were tugging at the backs of each other's shirts, or slipping their arms out of their sleeves to twist their shirts backwards to check their labels. They struggled to pronounce, "Lesotho! Indonesia! Pakistan! Honduras!" and quickly started making connections: "Pablo, my shirt is from your country, El Salvador! Tran, my sneakers are from Vietnam! Maria, Steven's sweater is from Ecuador!"

We pulled out world maps and globes to find the continents where these countries were located. We made a quick bar graph and started to analyze it. The children wanted to know why most sneakers come from Asian countries. They wondered why hardly anything was made in the United States and why nothing had a union label. Where did the union label go?

With this enthusiasm for clothing manufacture, instead of using "lost teeth data" for my planned math unit, I decided to adapt clothing data to teach the same skills. I gave the students a homework assignment to learn categories their families use to sort dirty laundry (light/dark, clean/dirty, on the floor/in the drawers). Their next assignment was to help sort laundry and record label data—including country of manufacture—from one load of wash. Data came flooding in. We developed a color-coding system to sort the countries by continent and groups made six-foot-tall graphs to show where our clothing was made.

This led to social studies, where we learned about the economics of labor. I read books such as *Sí, Se Puede!* (the SEIU Justice for Janitors campaign in Los Angeles), *Harvest of Hope* (biography of Cesar Chavez), *Farmer Duck, Swimmy,* and *Click, Clack, Moo: Cows That Type.* I gave homework assignments asking parents/guardians to share stories about relatives or ancestors who worked in clothing or textile factories, belonged to unions, and/or knew anything about the silk, button, or other textile industry. We began learning about the drive to organize textile and garment workers; how unions improved hours, wages, and safety; and how garment manufacturers started to move their factories south and then overseas in search of cheaper labor.

During morning meeting, we followed an impending supermarket workers' strike and discussed news clippings that students brought in about labor issues. A parent who had been involved with labor organizing in Korean clothing factories came in to talk about working conditions abroad and the meaning of fair trade.

We went to the computer lab to watch a video clip of the original *Look for the Union Label* commercial. We learned it was one of the most successful television commercials in the history of American marketing campaigns. My students wanted to learn the song, so we did that in morning meeting, with props for vocabulary such as *blouse* and *wages* to support our English language learners. The children wanted to film their commercial, so I recruited a former student who borrowed equipment from the high school to film and edit it.

We took a field trip to the Ten Thousand Villages store to learn more about free-trade products in our community.

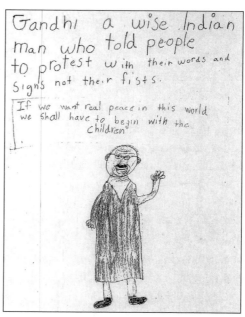

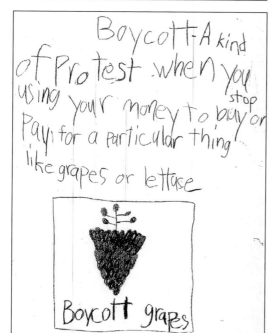

We met with the economic development officer at City Hall to find out where the clothing manufacturing jobs in our city went.

During Writing Workshop, a student proposed that we write and illustrate a *Protesters' Dictionary* to help other kids understand these issues. We set to work reading and writing to support the development of our dictionary, which included entries such as *boycott, union, Gandhi, negotiation, product,* and *health benefits.*

What began as a quest to find where our shirts were made became curriculum across content areas. Passionate in their investigations, the students learned a great deal as our study spread across language arts, math, geography, and economics; into our families and community; and across the globe.

Mary's Journey: Pathways to Enacting These Practices

A cornerstone of my teaching that has led me to the practices described here is the belief that education is about helping students develop as informed citizens who can make a difference in the world. To do this, I recognize that they need to become proficient in specific literacy skills and strategies, but I also know that they can learn those skills while engaged in experiences that are meaningful to them and that support their growth as critical thinkers.

Teaching in this way does not mean that I ignore standards and other guidelines. However, it does mean that I am not constrained by them. I have come to see standards in much the same way that I came to understand the varieties and power of biblical interpretation during my community organizing days. As a community organizer for fourteen years before becoming a teacher, I attended services at dozens of churches to pitch for funds, recruit volunteers, kick off a food drive, or deliver a eulogy. One thing I learned was the astounding variety of biblical interpretations. I heard scores of different messages, from a broad range of spiritual traditions, all out of one book. I see standards in much the same way—open to multiple interpretations that depend on the teacher, the teacher's knowledge of his or her students, and on the teacher's commitment to supporting the communities in which students live. One might see the vignette from my classroom as an illustration of what I call "biblical interpretation of the standards."

I strongly believe that interpreting standards based on the needs, knowledge, and communities of one's own students is essential. I worry about educators who feel that standards are "the truth, the whole truth, and nothing but the truth." I worry that too many teachers are frightened away from teaching anything that isn't packaged, scripted, mandated, or tested. By telling our own teaching stories, we can empower each other to use standards as points of departure for integrating curriculum, supporting student inquiry, and teaching critically. For example, the civics standard for first grade says to teach that "laws and rules are to keep us safe." This provides a perfect opportunity to teach about the role we each can play in ensuring that laws keep us safe, using examples of civil disobedience that changed the world such as the Montgomery bus boycott and Gandhi's salt march to the sea. My point is not to "cover" standards but to find a way to give my students the opportunity to actually use each skill in a real-world (vs. a worksheet) way.

Using standards as a point of departure for critical teaching also means that, as educators, we must continue to build our professional knowledge so that we know when it's important to take action to revise standards that are not supportive of great teaching. So, I make myself thoroughly aware of standards and use them to support my knowledge that comes from many other sources: professional reading, experience, deep involvement with families and communities, and convictions about how teaching can contribute to the growth of human beings who have the potential to make the world a better place.

⊚ *Pláticas Literarias/* Small-Group Literature Discussions

by Julia López-Robertson

Meet the Teacher

For fourteen years, I was a bilingual primary teacher at a Title I elementary school in Tucson, Arizona. The school serves preschool through grade 5 and is located in an urban working-class neighborhood. Of the approximately 650 children attending the school at that time, 95 percent of them were classified as English language learners, 98 percent received free lunch, and 2 percent qualified for reduced-price lunch. The school sits amid single-family homes, churches, businesses, a Catholic school, and a couple of apartment complexes. There were twenty children in my second-grade class. All of them were bilingual (Spanish-English) and self-identified as either Mexican or Mexican American. The bilingual model in the school was a maintenance model, meaning that there was a commitment to supporting the maintenance of home languages while adding English proficiency. Prior to teaching primary grades, I worked as a bilingual reading specialist for the district, and I have a master's degree in bilingual education. Before that, I taught special education for a year and prior to that, I taught at a Catholic Elementary School in Boston.

Teaching and Learning Moments in Julia's Classroom

I was running late to school one day and, as I made it to the crosswalk on Estrella Street, I noticed that Señora Randón (all names are pseudonyms), our crossing guard, had something tucked under her left arm while she held up the stop sign in her right hand. Curious, I followed her with my eyes as she made her way back up on the sidewalk. I watched as she took the object out from under her arm and walked toward a group of ladies sitting in lawn chairs. On further inspection, I saw Señoras Villa, Ramirez, Salvo, and Montserrat. They were mothers of five of my Latina students. Then I saw what she had in her hand; it was a children's book. I had to know what was going on so I turned the corner, pulled up alongside the ladies, and asked them what they were doing:

JULIA: ¡Buenos días, Señoras! ¿Qué hacen?

Good morning, Ladies. What are you doing?

SRA. R: ¡Pues, Mis, estamos haciendo nuestra tarea!

Well, Miss, we are doing our homework! [laughing]

JULIA:	Disculpen, Señoras, pero, ¿cuál tarea?	*Pardon me, ladies, What homework?*
SRA. M:	Pues, la que nos puso.	*Well, the one you gave us.*
SRA. S:	Sí, pues los libros, Mis, estamos leyendo nuestros libros. Y ahora vamos a hablar de ellos.	*Yes, well the books, Miss, we are reading our books. Then we will talk about them.*
SRA. R:	Y cuando terminemos, vamos a escribir en nuestro cuaderno, ¿vez?	*And when we are finished, we will write in our journals, see?*

[The mothers hold up the journals that I had given their daughters, my students.]

JULIA:	¿Y quién les dijo de esta tarea?	*And, who told you about this homework?*
TODAS:	¡Las chiquitas!	*The little ones [girls].*
JULIA:	¡Las chiquitas! ¿Si no les molesta, exactamente qué fue lo que le dijeron?	*The girls! If you don't mind, what exactly did they tell you?*
SRA. V:	Pues, que usted dijo que teníamos que leer y escribir como ellas.	*Well, that you told us that we had to read and write like they were.*
SRA. M:	Y como que somos niñas tan buenas, aquí estamos haciendo nuestra tarea.	*And because we are such good girls, here we are doing our homework. [laughing]*

I was not typically late for school, but that morning I was thrilled that I had been delayed! Stopping to talk to mothers of my students allowed me to see that the *pláticas literarias*—small-group literature discussions—in my classroom were making a difference not only at school but also at home. Twice weekly, I met with my second graders in small groups to discuss books. Sometimes the books were chosen by the students, but often I selected books from a collection of texts relevant to their cultural and linguistic backgrounds. I wanted to capitalize on their knowledge and experience while helping them learn about the structure, vocabulary, and uses of literacy.

The small-group *pláticas* typically took place on Wednesdays and Fridays. I prepared the students by reading the books aloud (in Spanish and in English) to the whole class on Mondays and Tuesdays. Following these read-alouds, we had whole-class discussions focused on conventions, vocabulary, and other reading skills and strategies that were necessary to make sense of the text. Students shared words they found interesting or challenging and I noted them on a large piece of butcher paper. This became part of our word wall and was used as a resource when the children were reading and/or writing. An interesting aspect of these lessons was what

I learned—words in Spanish that the children used but that were unfamiliar to me (and vice versa).

The focus of the small-group *pláticas* was somewhat different. I wanted to create a space where children felt safe to explore issues and experiences that might be

difficult for them in the larger group. I chose books that contained social issues that had affected some of the families: racism, immigration, language, and literacy. Because these discussions drew on matters that were familiar to the children, they were able to discuss and question social issues that were significant to them.

I often invited the families to participate in similar discussions at home, prior to discussing the books at school, because I believe that the family is a child's first teacher and I respect the resources that our children bring from their homes. During these home discussions, the children were asked to label three to five parts in the book that the children wished to discuss at

school. They were also asked to write a journal entry containing questions, thoughts, wonderings, and/or connections with the book. Figure 4.1 is an excerpt from seven-year-old Kati's response to reading *Radio Man* by Arthur Dorros.

When I talked with the mothers on the street corner that morning, I found out that their daughters had decided that they needed to participate in the discussions just like we did at school. From that moment, I began encouraging families to provide written responses as well as to support their children's responses. Mothers'

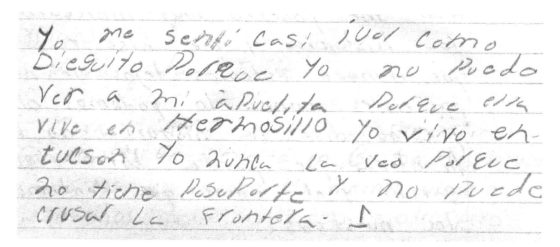

FIGURE 4.1: Kati's journal response to *Radio Man:* "I felt almost the same as Dieguito because I can't see my grandmother because she lives in Hermosillo [and] I live in Tucson. I never see her because she doesn't have a passport and she can't cross the border."

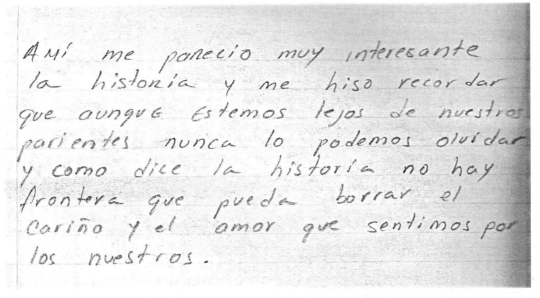

FIGURE 4.2: Sra. Salvo's response to her daughter's reading responses: "I thought the story was very interesting and it reminded me that even though we are far away from our families, we can never forget them and, just as the story says, there is no border that can erase the warmth and love that we feel for our own."

responses, like Sra. Salvo's in Figure 4.2, not only provided excellent models for the children but also gave me tremendous insights into the challenges, issues, and joys experienced at home.

This kind of community connection made a huge difference in my teaching. Through these relationships with family members—on the school corner and as I visited their homes and was invited to family gatherings—we developed a trust in each other. We worked together in support of their children's learning. There was no room for me to make inaccurate assumptions about my students' families. I knew them well enough to know that they loved and cared for their children, so I was able to erase stereotypes about their lack of support for the children's learning. I learned that support wasn't necessarily tied to parents coming to school, but that they cared deeply about their children's education and joined them in the study of books at home (or on the street corner) with great seriousness and respect for learning.

Julia's Journey: Pathways to Enacting These Practices

As an elementary school teacher, I had the privilege of teaching students who brought their rich languages and heritage to my classroom. It was important for me to (a) show children that I valued their languages and heritage, (b) spend time in their communities so I could learn more about their worlds, (c) engage students in reading books that reflected as well as extended their worlds, and (d) engage the families in our discussions of literature. Books became an entrée for me into their lives, a way to connect as well as to teach.

The time I spent getting to know children through book discussions and in their homes was probably the most valuable time spent in support of my ability to make instructional decisions. It also allowed me to develop a trust that was integral to my own learning—I had moved to Tucson from Boston and knew close to nothing about the desert or the Mexican culture. I relied on my students and their families to teach me, and teach me they did!

I created curriculum based on what I learned from my students and their families. Then, I aligned the curriculum with required standards. That alignment was never difficult because, teaching in this way, the standards just fell into place. By implementing the *pláticas literarias*, the children were required to read, think critically, learn conventions of print and how to make meaning from text, deepen vocabulary, write, formulate and support opinions, listen to others, and make textual connections. This addressed multiple standards while taking our learning and my insights about the children far beyond them.

Charting the Practice in Second Grade

Have a look at some of the teaching/learning moments in Nancy's, Mary's, and Julia's classrooms. The chart asks you to consider how these moments address some principles that NCTE has identified as foundational to great teaching while meeting several Common Core State Standards.

NCTE Principles and Beliefs	Teaching/Learning Moments in Nancy's Classroom	Teaching/Learning Moments in Mary's Classroom	Teaching/Learning Moments in Julia's Classroom
Home cultures and languages should be celebrated and used as foundational to instruction, as well as learning about cultures beyond the students' own. *Readers use life experiences, their knowledge of the topic, and their knowledge of oral and written language to make sense of print.*	The children take home disposable cameras and bring back photos that motivate their poetry writing. Nancy teaches a mini-lesson to demonstrate how she used her own photo to support her writing. The children's poetry celebrates the important people and experiences in their lives.	Children use maps and globes to identify where their clothes are made. This initiates reading and writing about clothing manufacture. Students complete a graph of clothing manufacture after conducting a survey based on research into their home laundry sorting.	Julia reads aloud in both Spanish and English. Literature discussion groups read bilingual texts. Books reflect immigration experiences familiar to the children. Julia invites families to engage in their own literature discussions, which, in turn, support the students.
Books and other texts are important tools to use in demonstrations of skills, conventions, and craft elements in the teaching of writing.	The classroom is filled with books of all kinds, including poetry and photography books. They are used for mini-lessons— "What did you notice about the poetry books?"—and as resources as students write.	Mary uses a range of texts—books, a song, speakers, newspapers, field trips, and websites—to teach about labor issues. In the process, students learn about nonfiction reading and writing.	Julia uses literature discussion groups to demonstrate what readers do as they critically analyze text and to introduce elements of writing used by the authors of children's books.
Children learn vocabulary, word patterns, letter-sound correspondences, and conventions and understanding of literary craft best when they are supported in doing so explicitly, yet in the context of meaningful oral and print experiences.	As they read, write, and talk about poetry, students extend vocabulary, grow as spellers, and understand more about the structure of language. Nancy uses a T-chart to teach differences between poetic and scientific language. Students apply the T-chart lesson in their own writing.	Students expand knowledge of vocabulary, how to present information, and other literacy conventions as they develop the *Protester's Dictionary.*	Students learn new vocabulary, reading strategies, and word structures and they learn to take a critical stance in their book discussions.

Where do you see these Common Core State Standards supported in Nancy's, Mary's, and Julia's vignettes?

Speaking and Listening

- Standard SL.2.1. Participate in collaborative conversations with diverse partners about *grade 2 topics and texts* with peers and adults in small and larger groups.
  - Follow agreed-upon rules for discussions (e.g., gaining the floor in respectful ways, listening to others with care, speaking one at a time about the topics and texts under discussion).
  - Build on others' talk in conversations by linking their comments to the remarks of others.
  - Ask for clarification and further explanation as needed about the topics and texts under discussion.
- Standard SL.2.2. Recount or describe key ideas or details from a text read aloud or information presented orally or through other media.
- Standard SL.2.3. Ask and answer questions about what a speaker says in order to clarify comprehension, gather additional information, or deepen understanding of a topic or issue.

Reading: Literature

- Standard RL.2.1. Ask and answer such questions as *who, what, where, when, why*, and *how* to demonstrate understanding of key details in a text.
- Standard RL.2.3. Describe how characters in a story respond to major events and challenges.
- Standard RL.2.4. Describe how words and phrases (e.g., regular beats, alliteration, rhymes, repeated lines) supply rhythm and meaning in a story, poem, or song.
- Standard RL.2.5. Describe the overall structure of a story, including describing how the beginning introduces the story and the ending concludes the action.
- Standard RL.2.6. Acknowledge differences in the points of view of characters, including by speaking in a different voice for each character when reading dialogue aloud.

Reading: Informational Text

- Standard RI.2.1. Ask and answer such questions as *who, what, where, when, why*, and *how* to demonstrate understanding of key details in a text.
- Standard RI.2.4. Determine the meaning of words and phrases in a text relevant to a *grade 2 topic or subject area*.
- Standard RI.2.6. Know and use various text features (e.g., captions, bold print, subheadings, glossaries, indexes, electronic menus, icons) to locate key facts or information in a text efficiently.
- Standard RI.2.7. Explain how specific images (e.g., a diagram showing how a machine works) contribute to and clarify a text.
- Standard RI.2.8. Describe how reasons support specific points the author makes in a text.
- Standard RI.2.9. Compare and contrast the most important points presented by two texts on the same topic.

Reading: Foundational Skills

- Standard RF.2.4. Read with sufficient accuracy and fluency to support comprehension.
  - Read grade-level text with purpose and understanding.
  - Read grade-level text orally with accuracy, appropriate rate, and expression.
  - Use context to confirm or self-correct word recognition and understanding, rereading as necessary.

Writing

- Standard W.2.2. Write informative/explanatory texts in which they introduce a topic, use facts and definitions to develop points, and provide a concluding statement or section.

- Standard W.2.3. Write narratives in which they recount a well-elaborated event or short sequence of events, include details to describe actions, thoughts, and feelings, use temporal words to signal event order, and provide a sense of closure.

- Standard W.2.5. With guidance and support from adults and peers, focus on a topic and strengthen writing as needed by revising and editing.

- Standard W.2.6. With guidance and support from adults, use a variety of digital tools to produce and publish writing, including in collaboration with peers.

- Standard W.2.7. Participate in shared research and writing projects (e.g., read a number of books on a single topic to produce a report; record science observations).

- Standard W.2.8. Recall information from experiences or gather information from provided sources to answer a question.

Language

- Standard L.2.5. Demonstrate understanding of figurative language, word relationships and nuances in word meanings.
  - Identify real-life connections between words and their use (e.g., *describe foods that are spicy or juicy*).
  - Distinguish shades of meaning among closely related verbs (e.g., *toss, throw, hurl*) and closely related adjectives (e.g., *thin, slender, skinny, scrawny*).

- Standard L.2.6. Use words and phrases acquired through conversations, reading and being read to, and responding to texts, including using adjectives and adverbs to describe (e.g., *When other kids are happy that makes me happy*).

5

Learning Literacy through Inquiries in a Multiage Primary Classroom

◎ Of Runaways and Bug Hospitals

by Freida Hammett

Meet the Teacher

I have been a teacher and media specialist for more than twenty-five years. Currently, I teach a multiage first-, second-, and third-grade class in an elementary school just inside the city limits of Atlanta, Georgia. My class this year is made up of twenty-five children and reflects the diversity of the school: African American, Latino, African, Korean, Asian, Indian, Arabic, and European American. I am excited that my class-room represents different ways of being in the world. A belief foundational to my teaching is that the children and I learn about how language works within and across diverse com-munities. This year, for example, one family shared their Hindu beliefs surrounding the festival of Diwali and another family taught us about the Amharic calendar used in parts of Ethiopia. I also ask family members to teach us words and phrases in their home languages so that, during morning meeting, we can greet each other in Spanish, Amharic, Korean, Hindi, and Arabic as well as English.

When you walk into my classroom, you will experience another foundation of my teaching: My students—six-, seven-, and eight-year-olds—are typically work-ing together as they engage in themes or inquiries generated from their interests as well as from curricular guides. I find that the children learn to read, write, research, and learn content better when the work is driven by their fascinations. I meet the students' individual needs through small-group instruction and one-to-one confer-ences. In the vignette that follows, my students are engaged in just such an inquiry, one that grew from our fascination with insects.

Teaching and Learning Moments in Freida's Classroom

If you were in our school courtyard this fall, you couldn't help but notice orange-and-black Gulf Fritillary butterflies flitting through the garden. If you took note of the plants and the critters on them, you would have noticed orange-and-black striped caterpillars. Looking at the parsley and dill, you might have spotted yellow, green, and black caterpillars. By October, the students in my classroom had seen six different caterpillars and identified four of them. The *National Audubon Society Field Guide to North American Butterflies* and its companion text, *Field Guide to Insects*, flew off the classroom shelves as students sought

Other resources can be found online at websites such as http://www.enature.com.

to identify and learn about the caterpillars. They discovered Swallowtails on parsley and dill, Gulf Fritillaries on the passion fruit plant, and Monarchs on the milkweed plants. We placed them in our classroom Butterfly House and every day watched with fascination. During read-alouds, independent reading, writing workshop, and scientific investigations, we pursued and expressed information to support our curiosities. In the process, the children learned a lot about a range of literacies, practiced reading and writing informational texts, and explored scientific concepts. But let me tell you how that learning started.

Observations of insects, animals, reptiles, or birds can evolve into similar learning experiences (see Whitin & Whitin, 1997).

One day as I left the classroom, I forgot something very important—to zip closed the Butterfly House! The next day, we noticed right away that our Monarch caterpillars had escaped, run away, flown the coop! We couldn't find them. Students suggested all kinds of hypotheses: "Maybe they changed into butterflies already!" "Maybe they crawled out the door!"

For tips on inexpensive ways to build your own classroom butterfly house, visit http://www.butterflyschool.org/teacher/makehouse.html.

Soon I discovered one runaway crawling on the floor. I gently put it back in the Butterfly House, where it munched its way through milkweed leaves. But where was the other one? We looked high and low. No caterpillar of that stripe could be found in the classroom. Then, one sharp-eyed boy discovered a gorgeous green chrysalis with golden dots hanging from our mat basket—could it be our missing Monarch? Every day, we observed the chrysalis, marveling at its beauty and transformation.

In the meantime, two students decided to make a Bug Hospital. They planned what should go in it and who would make it. Within a few days, we had an extensive hospital, complete with a Caterpillar House or, more appropriate to a hospital, a nursery ward.

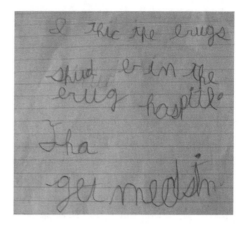

In preparing to make their arguments, students could also make lists of pros and cons for each argument and try using an interactive persuasion map, such as the one available at http://www.readwritethink.org/files/resources/interactives/persuasion_map/. For a printable map, visit http://www.readwritethink.org/files/resources/printouts/persuasion%20map.pdf.

At about that time, the students found a grasshopper with four legs. Using our field guides, we studied the narrative text, illustrations, and diagrams and learned that grasshoppers are insects and that all insects have six legs. The grasshopper was missing two legs! Some of the children thought the grasshopper should go in the hospital. Others said, "No! It should stay in its habitat!" This led to a study of how to develop persuasive arguments. Each student took a passionate position and developed a rationale—verbally and in writing—about where the grasshopper should be placed. After sharing their positions through a heated debate, it was decided that the grasshopper would be put in the hospital.

I was not looking forward to the next day, fearing I would discover a dead grasshopper. But the next morning brought a surprise—the grasshopper had checked itself out of the bug hospital and more patients had admitted themselves! First there was a Variegated Fritillary that had a damaged

wing. Could it be from the chrysalis we had watched so closely? We quickly began to use our knowledge and our textual resources to develop a hypothesis about how the damage might have occurred.

The interest in these creatures led to self-directed research and further writing: a report on grasshoppers, several on black widow spiders (prompted by finding one just outside the building), and discussions on the poison potential of daddy-long-legs. The field guides to insects and butterflies stayed in student hands all day. Several students made books about butterflies, their own versions of the field guides. Others made booklets about the parts of grasshoppers or spiders. To support their writing, the students referred to our classroom library of informational texts and I taught them to use illustrations, diagrams, text headings, tables of contents, and glossaries, not only to locate information but also to create their own texts.

For students who were in the early stages of learning to write, I encouraged the use of a movable alphabet—individual letters housed in a large box. When using a movable alphabet, students think through each word they want to write, pull the appropriate letters, and arrange them on a floor mat. We call this their rough draft. After their writing gets checked for revisions, they copy the work on paper. As students completed drafts, they excitedly shared their insect stories with one another.

We now have nine chrysalides in the Bug House, representing four different varieties. Just today, a new Monarch emerged, so we've had birth as well as death. We've also witnessed "murder" in the courtyard when we saw a stinkbug sucking the juice from an unidentified caterpillar. Most important, we have seen life cycles close up, becoming thrilled in the process. We learned about literacies while exploring the real life-and-death dramas of the insect kingdom.

Japanese Emperor Polyphemus moth

Freida's Journey: Pathways to Enacting These Practices

Long ago, I developed the belief that children learn more when they see purpose in their learning—not *my* purpose, *their* purpose. Over the years, I have worked through how to teach with that in mind. By trying out new ideas, attending professional conferences, talking through ideas with colleagues, and taking graduate courses, I've come to believe that it is my responsibility to develop a classroom environment that intentionally provokes interest. To be able to do this, I know that I must pay close attention to the kinds of things that interest the children. I need to understand literacy well enough to know what

> If you don't have a movable alphabet, students could create their own by writing letters on construction paper, cutting them into small squares, and laminating them. Plastic or magnetic letters are also great for this.

children need to learn to develop as readers and writers. And I need to be able to use that knowledge to create instructional experiences that move each child forward. To support this style of teaching, I must also ensure that my room is filled with resources, including a large collection of children's books in English and in other languages, and that we take advantage of a well-stocked school library, the school's computer center, and the environment around us.

My whole philosophy of teaching can be summed up as: *Follow the child*. Over the years, it's become clear to me that I can guide children in learning skills by relating those skills to their interests. I bring this same approach to the way that I incorporate state standards in my teaching. I ask questions such as, What does this child need in order to progress? Which standards will help me focus on those needs? Which standards are most important for my students? In this way, I use the children's needs to prioritize my approach to the standards. As a result, I am able to coordinate the standards with the activities going on in the classroom with relative ease. And, perhaps more important, I am able to accomplish this without losing focus on what matters most—my students.

I suppose it all boils down to knowing the standards and then finding ways of making them fit a particular learning situation. Rather than starting with the standards and then planning an activity, I believe it is important to focus on children's interests first. With the project involving insects, I was familiar enough with the standards to know how I could address a number of them in each activity. As we moved through an activity, I allowed the children to lead the way and I followed with a checklist in my head of what they needed to learn and how the standards were being realized. This way, I guided the children's work to meet standards while constantly recognizing and adapting to their needs. In my classroom, the children and I drive the standards, rather than being driven by them. This makes for a much happier and enjoyable place!

The bottom line is that I believe strongly in the ability of each child to succeed. I believe that each one of my students will find his or her particular role to fulfill in this world. This is dependent on how school experiences help students build confidence in envisioning possibilities *and* the skills and ability to bring these possibilities to life. The Common Core State Standards provide one means through which I can gauge my ability to help students accomplish these goals.

Charting the Practice in a Grades 1–3 Multiage Classroom

Charting the practice in Freida's multiaged classroom, we tried a different approach to be able to capture ways that multiage teaching addresses grade-level standards without separating the children into first-, second-, and third-grade groups for instruction. Freida's teaching moments are charted adjacent to standards addressed at each grade level. NCTE principles are listed at the bottom of the chart.

Teaching/Learning Moments in Freida's Classroom	Standards Addressed Grade 1	Standards Addressed Grade 2	Standards Addressed Grade 3
	Reading: Foundational Skills		
To gain knowledge about butterflies and insects, Freida reads aloud and students read a wide variety of informational texts.	4. Read with sufficient accuracy and fluency to support comprehension. • Read texts with purpose and understanding. • Read texts orally with accuracy and expression. • Use context to confirm or self-correct.	4. Read with sufficient accuracy and fluency to support comprehension. • Read texts with purpose and understanding. • Read texts orally with accuracy and expression. • Use context to confirm or self-correct.	4. Read with sufficient accuracy and fluency to support comprehension. • Read with purpose and understanding. • Read prose and poetry with accuracy and expression. • Use context to confirm or self-correct.
	Reading: Informational Text		
The classroom library is filled with nonfiction texts as well as other books relevant to students' interests and to the study of butterflies and other insects.	10. With prompting and support, read informational texts appropriately complex for grade 1.	10. Read and comprehend informational texts in the grades 2–3 text complexity band proficiently, with scaffolding as needed at the high end of the range.	10. Read and comprehend informational texts, at the high end of the grades 2–3 text complexity band independently and proficiently.

Connections to NCTE Principles and Beliefs

- Students read a wide range of print and non-print texts to build an understanding of texts, of themselves, and of the cultures of the United States and the world; to acquire new information; to respond to the needs and demands of society and the workplace; and for personal fulfillment. Among these texts are fiction and nonfiction, classic and contemporary works.
- Students read a wide range of literature from many periods in many genres to build an understanding of the many dimensions (e.g., philosophical, ethical, aesthetic) of human experience.

Teaching/Learning Teaching Moments in Freida's Classroom	Standards Addressed Grade 1	Standards Addressed Grade 2	Standards Addressed Grade 3
	Writing		
Students observe the caterpillars in the Butterfly House and the Bug Hospital and report their findings to each other and to Freida.	8. With guidance and support from adults, recall information from experiences or gather information from provided sources to answer a question.	8. Recall information from experiences or gather information from provided sources to answer a question.	8. Recall information from experiences or gather information from print and digital sources; take brief notes on sources and sort evidence into provided categories.
Students conduct self-directed research.	7. Participate in shared research and writing projects.	7. Participate in shared research and writing projects.	7. Conduct short research projects that build knowledge about a topic.
Students develop and write persuasive arguments for or against putting the insects in the Bug Hospital.	1. Write opinion pieces in which they introduce the topic or name the book they are writing about, state an opinion, supply a reason for the opinion, and provide some sense of closure.	1. Write opinion pieces, state an opinion, supply reasons that support the opinion, use linking words to connect opinion and reasons, and provide a concluding statement or section.	1. Write opinion pieces: • Introduce the topic, state an opinion. • Support the opinion. • Use linking words and phrases to connect opinion and reasons. • Provide conclusion.
Students create reports and field guides based on their content learning. 1–1 conferences with Freida move students' writing forward.	5. With guidance and support from adults, focus on a topic, respond to suggestions from peers, and add details to strengthen writing as needed.	5. With guidance and support from adults and peers, focus on a topic and strengthen writing as needed by revising and editing.	5. With guidance and support from peers and adults, develop and strengthen writing as needed by planning, revising, and editing.

Connections to NCTE Principles and Beliefs

- Students apply a wide range of strategies to comprehend, interpret, evaluate, and appreciate texts. They draw on prior experience, interactions with other readers and writers, knowledge of word meaning and other texts, word identification strategies, and understanding of textual features.

- Students employ a wide range of strategies as they write and use different writing process elements appropriately to communicate with different audiences for a variety of purposes.

- Students conduct research on issues and interests by generating ideas and questions, and by posing problems. They gather, evaluate, and synthesize data from a variety of sources to communicate their discoveries in ways that suit their purpose and audience.

- Students use a variety of technological and information resources to gather and synthesize information and to create and communicate knowledge.

Teaching/Learning Teaching Moments in Freida's Classroom	Standards Addressed Grade 1	Standards Addressed Grade 2	Standards Addressed Grade 3
	Speaking and Listening		
Students and teacher discuss multiple issues, concerns, information, plans, etc. related to their topics of inquiry and concern for the insects in their care.	1. Participate in collaborative conversations in small and large groups.	1. Participate in collaborative conversations with diverse partners about grade 2 topics and texts with peers and adults in small and larger groups.	1. Engage effectively in a range of collaborative discussions building on others' ideas and expressing their own. • Come to discussions having studied required material; draw on that preparation to explore ideas.
Students present their learning through oral reports.	4. Describe people, places, things, and events with relevant details, expressing ideas and feelings clearly.	4. Tell a story or recount an experience with appropriate facts and relevant, descriptive details, speaking audibly in coherent sentences.	4. Report on a topic or text, tell a story, or recount an experience with appropriate facts and relevant, descriptive details, speaking clearly at an understandable pace.

Connections to NCTE Principles and Beliefs

- Students adjust their use of spoken, written, and visual language to communicate effectively with a variety of audiences and for different purposes.
- Students apply knowledge of language structure, language conventions, media techniques, figurative language, and genre to create, critique, and discuss print and non-print texts.
- Students participate as knowledgeable, reflective, creative, and critical members of a variety of literacy communities.
- Students use spoken, written, and visual language to accomplish their own purposes.

⊚ Conclusion to Section II

Obstacles and Challenges

Mariel, Tammy, Janice, Carmen, Jessica, Nancy, Mary, Julia, and Freida are wonderful teachers who put standards in perspective knowing that their professional knowledge and knowledge of each child are key to successful teaching. They share a commitment to engaging students in learning about and through literacies and languages in many forms. They work to continuously deepen their understandings about how to help students grow as proficient, passionate, and critical producers and consumers of literacies.

But their paths to teaching in these ways are not without obstacles and challenges. Like you, they would be the first to say that they have moments of frustration as well as success every day. They also know that some obstacles can lead to frustration that is difficult to overcome. For this reason, the vignette teachers share a few of their challenges along with strategies they use to address them (Table 5.1), hoping to validate others' frustrations while providing suggestions for addressing obstacles and moving beyond them.

TABLE 5.1: Obstacles and Challenges Experienced by Vignette Teachers and Strategies They Used to Address Those Challenges

Obstacle or Challenge	Strategies Used to Address the Obstacle
Writing to Prompts: Our district wants us to use a scripted writing program relying on prompts, but I know that students do not learn to write well when they are given a steady diet of prompts.	I share examples of children's work over time (to show progress) at inservice meetings and with my principal. In this way, I can show that when my students have opportunities to write from the heart, based on their real experiences, their writing is so much better than when they write to a prompt. I also show how I teach tested skills—grammar, sentence structure, spelling, expression, and organization of ideas—using students' from-the-heart writing. I explain that I don't neglect prompt writing (because I want my students to do well on district tests), but first I teach my students to write; then I teach them how to transfer that knowledge to the testing genre.
Skills in Isolation: We are required to follow district pacing guides, where everything is broken down separately, but I feel that an integrated approach would be much more effective.	I overcome this by building my own confidence through professional study. When I can articulate why an integrated approach works *and* I have student work to demonstrate impact of the approach, I can show how I address all of the skills in the pacing guide, but in ways that help students immediately connect the skills to real reading and writing.

Obstacle or Challenge	Strategies Used to Address the Obstacle
Organization: I find that not all obstacles are external. I was my own worst enemy in terms of organizing my time and making sure that I was in-the-moment with my students—not allowing the telephone, other teachers, or announcements from the office to interfere with my teaching.	It helped to get advice from a veteran teacher who was *extremely* organized. Even though her teaching approach was different from mine, I learned a lot from her. Also, once I *really* began to pay attention to how often I allowed interruptions to break the flow of my teaching, I was able to do a better job of avoiding them.
Negativity: I feel overwhelmed and disheartened by the undeserved negativity that I hear all the time about children and their families.	I try to interrupt negativity whenever I hear it by sharing examples of what I've learned that made me think differently. I also seek the company of teachers who genuinely value families and who don't bad-mouth them. I put myself in the company of colleagues I find to be positive.
Rumors: Hearing other teachers say things such as "The standards say you have to do it this way" or "You have to use these books" can send the wrong impression about what is actually allowed.	I make myself very familiar with our district guidelines. I want to see it in writing so I am not a victim of rumors. And I am careful not to buy into hearsay; I track everything back to the horse's mouth: Did someone actually say this? Is it in writing as policy? Or is it merely rumor or tradition?
Cultural Relevance: I don't feel like I always understand what is culturally relevant to my students.	When I spend time in my students' homes and communities—as a friend and colleague, not as an evaluator—I learn so much that helps me create curriculum. I can't get to every home right away, but over a year, I can. To make sure I am truly open to appreciating my students and their families, here are some things I try to do: • I ask, "What can families teach *me*?" • I think about other ways of doing things as just as legitimate as mine. • I go with families to community and family functions, even when I might be a little uncomfortable at first. • I turn on radio stations my kids listen to. I read about their favorite artists.
Support: When culturally relevant practices utilize materials and methods different from pacing guides and district-adopted materials, support is needed to use what works best for my students.	I assure everyone (administrators, families, children) that my teaching focuses on the best pathways to student achievement and I back that up by sharing articles and quotes from articles (because some people don't make time to read the whole article) and by keeping track of students' work so I can show the progress that is made.
Standardization: Some administrators want classrooms to look and sound like each other, which can make it difficult to teach to and through my students' interests, languages, and home knowledge.	I reassure administrators that I am covering required content, skills, and standards. I do this by making everything visible. For example, when I make a book with a rap song for literacy instruction, I include pages at the end that list the high-frequency words and tested skills (word patterns, contractions, compound words) that can be found in the book.

TABLE 5.1: Obstacles and Challenges Experienced by Vignette Teachers and Strategies They Used to Address Those Challenges *(continued)*

Obstacle or Challenge	Strategies Used to Address the Obstacle
Maintaining Enthusiasm: I find it difficult to maintain my enthusiasm for new ideas when everyone around me seems to be sinking into the status quo.	To stay enthusiastic, I need at least one like-minded colleague down the hall. So I find a partner who will work with me to stay abreast of the latest research. I also get involved in projects that the local university has to offer—research projects, supervising interns, conference opportunities, and listening to speakers.
Conferences: I don't know how to find funding to go to conferences or how to get release time to attend them.	Here are a few strategies I've used to get funding and time for conferences: • Get involved with a university project. Often professors are interested in learning with teachers and have funding to take them to conferences to present their work. • Do Internet searches for small grants from local and national sources. • Make a proposal to the district to conduct an inservice workshop after the conference. • Make a case for how conference attendance will affect student achievement.
Grade-Level Uniformity: I used to worry about how to plan with colleagues whose teaching is worksheet-based and who want everyone at our grade level to do the same thing.	At first, I accepted the worksheets with a smile, thanked colleagues for helping me, stuffed the worksheets in my desk drawer, and taught my students in a way that I felt was best. Now, because my colleagues know how I teach, they don't offer the worksheets much anymore.
Sharing What I Learn: I want to get more colleagues to be on board with more student-centered methods, joining professional organizations such as NCTE and WLU, and attending conferences.	I try to get colleagues on board by sharing what I've learned and telling them how exciting it is to present at conferences. I learn so much from them and I hope I can encourage more participation. I also notice that because my colleagues and I respect each other, we are influenced when we just hang out in each other's rooms and share ideas.

The Jumping-Off Point

We share these glimpses into the classrooms of nine teachers—their successes, obstacles, strategies, and journeys—as jumping-off points for reflection about your own classrooms as you consider teaching in a time of Common Core State Standards. We also share these classroom snapshots so that administrators and policymakers can see the kinds of teaching that become even stronger with administrative support in a time of standards. With these goals in mind, in the following section, we provide suggestions for focused reflection in support of the conversations that administrators, teachers, and policymakers must have as they work together to create educational environments of excellence for every child.

Planning the Big Picture

Focused Reflection, Planning, and Advocacy

6

I created curriculum based on what I learned from my students and their families. Then, I aligned the curriculum with required standards. That alignment was never difficult because, teaching in this way, the standards just fell into place. By implementing the *pláticas literarias,* the children were required to read, think critically, learn conventions of print and how to make meaning from text, deepen vocabulary, write, formulate and support opinions, listen to others, and make textual connections. This addressed multiple standards while taking our learning and my insights about the children far beyond them.

—JULIA LÓPEZ-ROBERTSON, SECOND-GRADE TEACHER

The classroom scenarios and professional reflections in Section II of this book provide a backdrop against which readers might consider their own instructional planning in a time of Common Core State Standards (or anytime). In the quote that opens this section, Julia describes how she planned the big picture in her second-grade classroom: she created structures to engage her students in thinking critically, embrace multiple ways of using languages and literacies, and teach specific skills and strategies. The big picture included attention to how easily standards would fall into place if she attended thoughtfully to the other elements of effective teaching.

In this section, we build from the Section II vignettes to explore ways that you (teachers, administrators, and policymakers) and your colleagues might think about standards as one part of the bigger picture. We see the big picture as encompassing three general areas around which this section is organized: (a) focused reflection/professional study (including suggestions for using Section II vignettes to support reflection), (b) planning for teaching, and (c) educational advocacy. We write to provide reflective and organizational possibilities for embracing the great work you already do while building knowledge that allows you to enhance and enact your visions of great teaching and your role as an advocate for teaching that makes a difference.

Focused Reflection in a Time of Common Core State Standards (or Anytime)

After more than twenty years in the classroom, kindergarten teacher Donna Jarvis said to a group of student teachers, "If I ever show signs of wanting to stop learning, I hope someone tells me it's time to call it a career" (Bell & Jarvis, 2002, p. 52). Like Donna, we believe that ongoing professional learning—focused reflection in professional learning communities—is key to great teaching and also to putting standards in perspective in light of current understandings in the field.

Decades of research demonstrate that the most effective support for teachers comes in the form of long-term study of both research and practice within learning communities that include administrators as well as teachers (Darling-Hammond, 1997; Donnelly et al., 2005). In reality, however, many teachers feel that opportunities for intellectual discussion are absent from much of the professional development offered in schools and districts. Thus, *particularly as we consider new standards*, it is essential that administrators and teachers prioritize the establishment of professional learning communities as powerful locations for collaboration and growth. As Darling-Hammond (2010) writes:

> If teachers, principals, and other professionals do not share up-to-date knowledge about effective practices, the field runs around in circles . . . many poor decisions are made and the efforts of those who are successful are continually undermined and counteracted by those who are uninformed and unskilled. (p. 196)

So, as you consider standards and wonder where to begin, we believe that instituting or revitalizing spaces for focused reflection in your schools and districts is an essential first step.

What might spaces for focused reflection look like?

Professional learning communities where focused reflection occurs can take a variety of forms. Key is to remember that opportunities for consistent, ongoing professional study are by far the most effective means of deepening educators' knowledge.

Jumping on the bandwagon of every professional development program that comes along makes it impossible for focused reflection to take place. When teachers are pushed and pulled in many directions—a book club on Mondays, a study group on Tuesdays, a grade-level meeting on Wednesdays, a district workshop on Thursdays—there can be no solid focus. The lack of consistency and focus makes it difficult to engage in the kind of deep learning that leads to growth. So, when we write about professional learning communities, we mean those that meet regularly and allow time for teachers and administrators to read; view videos and websites; attend local and national conferences; visit other schools (in and out of town/state); try out new ideas in their classrooms; and reflect, discuss, and evaluate those ideas with consistency of purpose over time.

Who will participate?

We believe that professional learning communities—spaces for study and reflection—that are most supportive of professional growth that affects student learning include the following:

- *Administrators as full participants* who read professional texts, participate in discussions, try out and evaluate new practices, and reflect in collaboration with classroom teachers.
- *Family and community members, teaching assistants, and other school personnel* who are typically overlooked when faculty study groups or book clubs are organized. (These members of the professional community provide essential insights and perspectives not possible without them, and they help schools become more inclusive, informed learning environments.)
- *A knowledgeable facilitator* with proven professional knowledge of culturally relevant literacy theory, assessment, and practice. (Representatives from companies selling programs are typically not the facilitators we are talking about.)

How do we get organized?

Begin by making time to meet. Plan your sessions so that professional study does not add to already overloaded schedules. Teachers and administrators make room for professional study by taking an honest look at how time is spent in schools and how resources (people and funding) are used. Ask yourselves hard questions about how those elements might be structured differently. Work together to identify what you need to let go of to make time for ongoing study, reflection, and growth.

Make a plan. It is a good idea to spend the first session talking through a trajectory for your group's experience—perhaps planning for nine weeks at a time. Consider what you want to accomplish. What will be the focus of your work? Maybe a topic came to mind as you read the vignettes in Section II or an issue or question sparked your curiosity from one of the discussions or resource lists in Section I. Think about how those topics, issues, and questions might interface with the needs you see in your school and classroom.

Once you've identified a focus, it helps to develop a time line that includes readings, videos, Web links for each session, and topics that will be discussed. This doesn't mean that you won't deviate from the plan if new directions present themselves, but it does provide a road map to keep you focused.

Establish a routine. Similarly, it is helpful to establish a routine for each meeting. Where will you meet? Will sessions involve food and drink? If so, who is responsible for bringing refreshments each week? Who is in charge of facilitating each meeting? Will you rotate that role? What is the responsibility of the facilitator? How will each meeting be structured?

One suggestion is to rotate locations from one session to the next so that each meeting takes places in a different teacher's classroom. This idea works beautifully when the group is contained within one school or when groups include educators from several schools. Group participants learn from seeing ways that new ideas are enacted across a range of classrooms, and they can provide celebrations as well as feedback that leads to further insights for the whole group.

What are some resources that could support our reflections?

As you plan for sessions across a period of time, it is helpful to develop a list of resources—professional books, journal articles, websites, videos, school visits—consistent with your focus. Suggestions for finding resources include the following:

- *The lists provided in the Section I textboxes and in the appendices of this book*: These lists were developed with teachers and administrators in mind. They are tried-and-true texts, videos, websites, and professional journals that we see as supportive of the work that teachers and administrators do, organized into themes or areas of inquiry that could easily become topics for study.

- *NCTE Squire's Office Policy Briefs*: Excellent encapsulations of key studies that support thoughtful practice can be found at http://www.ncte.org/policy-research/briefs. These concise, readable accounts of research provide excellent resources that can be used to build knowledge and to support the ability to articulate research behind the practice.

- *Websites of educational publishers*: Search for books that entice, but search with an educated eye so that you do not buy into every new source that appears in glossy brochures. Websites such as www.rethinkingschools.org; http://nameorg.org/resources; www.nabe.org/publications.html; www .heinemann.com; www.stenhouse.com; www.teacherscollegepress.com; and www.ncte.org/books can be good places to start.

- *Graduate course syllabi*: Have a look at the syllabi of professors from institutions of higher education that focus on the study of literacy education. Syllabi are often posted online and contain resource lists that can be focused and helpful. For example, early childhood educator Vivian Vasquez from American University has an extensive list of resources pertaining to critical literacy on her site, http://www.bazmakaz.com /criticalliteracy/about/. Many sites like this can be found from simple Internet searches.

- *Classrooms of inspirational teachers*: While reading, viewing videos, and watching podcasts or weblinks are informative, little can take the place of actually visiting other classrooms and interacting with other teachers. Making provisions for time and travel to visit exemplary classrooms is an important way that administrators and policymakers can give teachers access to new ideas and insights—opportunities to see, hear, feel, and question how ideas become a part of day-to-day life in schools.

How might we spend our time?

The following suggestions are provided to support the development of structures that allow for focused reflection and immediate connections to day-to-day teaching and student learning. One suggestion is to rotate meetings from classroom to classroom. Each session would be hosted by the facilitator and by the teacher in that classroom. With that possibility in mind (but also adaptable to other meeting plans), some ideas for structuring your time include the following:

- *Host teacher shares a book and an idea:* The host teacher takes responsibility for opening the session by sharing a piece of children's literature and then sharing an idea the teacher has been exploring in his or her classroom. The sharing might include video clips, student work samples, and/or newly constructed classroom centers, interest or inquiry areas, organization of texts, display of student work, etc. A helpful ground rule is that the ideas presented must connect to insights gained from the focus and content of the group's professional study—from readings/videos/Web links/school visits/ group discussions. This will help to maintain the group's focus and the connection between professional study and classroom practice.

- *Host teacher shares successes and challenges:* The host teacher then shares successes as well as challenges encountered in the exploration of this idea, posing questions that will help the group provide supportive feedback.

- *Group provides feedback:* The group provides celebrations (pointing out specific aspects of the host teacher's work that are impressive and/or that push group members' thinking in new ways); the group also provides feedback in response to challenges or questions raised.

- *Connecting to guiding principles and standards:* Then the group might look at the six guiding principles provided in Section I of this book as well as grade-level standards and consider how they are addressed as well as suggestions and further insights.

- *New discussion:* The group facilitator could then coordinate discussion about new readings, Web links, and video clips in relation to further implementation of ideas in classrooms.

- *Time to reflect:* Before concluding, participants might take a few minutes to capture insights from the session by writing brief reflections or reminders about what they want to try in their classrooms in the coming days and weeks and the standards they will address. This provides an initial plan and a reminder for teachers as they leave the session. It could be revisited at the beginning of the next session, as teachers share what they were able to accomplish in the past week(s).

While the preceding suggestions can be adapted for use in any professional learning community, a few general guidelines might be helpful as you create your own structure. No matter the venue, focus, or structure of your professional space, we suggest that at its foundation are opportunities to:

- *Build knowledge* by reading, discussing, making plans for trying out ideas in classrooms, and then sharing and evaluating those ideas in the company of colleagues.

- *Learn about family and community knowledge and languages* by involving family and community members as your instructors and curricular informants; their insights can also help you better understand students and how to support them.

- *Keep students at the center* by continuously asking: What does this article, video, Web link, idea, or theory mean for my classroom, my children, or a particular child tomorrow?

- *Review and assess student work together* to glean insights from each other about supporting individual children and groups of children.

- *Share ideas for instructional moments* that have been successful and those that have not been successful and seek advice from each other.

- *Share possibilities for future planning* and gather feedback and further suggestions.

- *Link to Section I guiding principles and standards* (for organization and easy reference, each teacher could keep a binder with dividers for Guiding Principles, Grade Level Standards, Articles, Reflections, and Plans).

How might we use the vignettes from Section II to support focused reflection?

The nine classroom vignettes in Section II provide a useful tool for focused reflection and a way to understand the breadth of possibility in a time of standards as those possibilities relate to your own school and classroom. Below, we offer questions to support reflection that builds from those vignettes. The questions are divided into themes that could be used as topics of study for your professional learning community.

Potential Topics of Study

Understanding Student Learning (Formative Assessment)

- Choose a favorite vignette. Choose one child in the vignette. Think about these questions:
  - What might the child be learning at this moment in time? What evidence leads you to assume that? What teaching decisions would you make based on that knowledge?
  - What more would you need to know to understand the child as a learner? How would you get that information?
  - How would you get to know the child's family and community so you could find out more about the knowledge the child brings to the classroom? How would you use that knowledge to inform further teaching?
  - Try this with another vignette, and another.

- List all of the assessment strategies demonstrated in these vignettes—the specific ways that the teachers learned about students as readers, writers, and language users. Then ask:
  - What did the teachers learn as a result of those assessment strategies?
  - How did they use that learning to make student expertise visible?
  - How did they use that learning to inform instruction?
  - What specific standards are addressed in the process?
  - In what ways do you use assessment to inform instruction? Are there new ideas you glean from the vignettes that will enhance your ability to understand children as readers and writers and use that knowledge to teach?
  - What do you want to know more about in terms of formative assessment? How might you access that knowledge?

Teaching Strategies

- Choose one or two vignettes. Generate a list of the teaching strategies used. How might you use these strategies in your own classroom? How would they look the same? How would they look different? How might you use those strategies to address specific standards?
- Turn to the list of six guiding principles in Section I of this book. Now reread one of the vignettes in Section II. Name the specific ways that the teaching embraces those six principles. Are there ways those principles might be further addressed? What insights does this reflection prompt with regard to your own teaching?
- What are some of the resources (knowledge, materials, student interests, home languages) these teachers call on to foster learning? Give specific examples of how these resources are used in vignette classrooms. How might you draw on similar resources to support learning in your classroom?

Valuing and Using Students' Home Knowledge

- How do these teachers demonstrate that they recognize and value diverse funds of knowledge possessed by students from a range of cultural and linguistic backgrounds? How do they use that knowledge to enhance their teaching?
- How do the teachers learn about and use students' families and communities as resources for teaching every child in the classroom? Give specific examples. How might you find out about and utilize similar resources in your classroom? What standards could you address in the process?

Language Diversity

- In what specific ways do the vignette teachers show respect for students' home languages? In what ways do they use those languages to promote classroom learning? What are some strategies from vignettes that you want to try related to bringing multiple languages into the classroom? How might you address standards in the process?

- In the vignettes, how do teachers who do not speak children's home languages figure out ways to make those languages a part of their classrooms? In what ways might this support learning for everyone?

- What languages, including African American Language (AAL), might your students and their families contribute to your classroom? What do you need to learn about those languages to be able to use them to foster learning? Who can help you with that learning? How might that help you address standards?

- What ideas from the list below might you access as you capitalize on home language resources while adding English proficiency to students' linguistic repertoires?

  - Ordering and using picture books and other materials that reflect home languages as well as English (see resource lists in Section I).

  - Creating texts with students and family members that reflect home languages and using them to foster bilingualism. For example, (a) multilingual labeling of the room, labels created collaboratively as you, family members, and children write together; (b) bilingual texts about children and their families, songs, and rhymes; and (c) read-alouds of bilingual texts placed at listening centers and on computers.

Culturally Relevant Practices

- Reread the overview of culturally relevant pedagogy in Section I. Use it to identify ways that vignette teachers are culturally responsive in their practices. Give specific examples and explain why they are culturally relevant using the criteria listed in the guiding principles (also in Section I). What else might the teachers do to further the culturally relevant nature of their teaching? How does this speak to you and your classroom? How might it help you address specific standards?

- With Section II vignettes in mind, think about the inclusive nature of teaching in your classroom/school. Are there some ways of being that dominate and others that may be left out of the curricular picture? You might begin by thinking in terms of language, ethnicity, family structure, and religion.

What changes might you make to further embrace multiple ways of being? How might those changes provide better learning opportunities and, in turn, address specific standards?

- What do you want to read next to understand more about culturally relevant literacy practices? See the textbox on page 18 in Section I for some suggestions of where you might start.

Critical Literacies and Problem Solving

- In what ways do teachers in the vignettes help students pay attention to a range of perspectives on specific issues, to consider what voices are included and left out of any piece of information, story, or account? Give specific examples.

- How do the teachers provide opportunities for students to think critically— to recognize the existence of multiple perspectives on particular ideas and issues—and to use that knowledge to solve problems and make a difference for others? How are students learning about literacy in the process? What standards are addressed?

- How do you engage students in similar ways? What might you consider in terms of adding a more critical foundation to your teaching?

Incorporating Technologies into Instruction

- What technologies do the vignette teachers use in their instruction? What further technologies might they use to enhance their teaching?

- How do these uses of technology foster student learning?

- What ideas do these reflections prompt for your own setting? What standards might you address through the use of technologies?

Charting Your Own Practice

In Section II, charts were provided that connected teaching/learning moments from the vignette classrooms with NCTE principles and beliefs and Common Core State Standards. Using the chart in Figure 6.1, or developing your own chart, try charting your own practice as an exercise in further reflection. One strategy for using this chart in your professional learning community is to share documentation of specific teaching/learning moments from your own classrooms (video clips, student work, photographs, etc.) and then work in grade-level teams or across

Teaching/ Learning Moment	How did I start with knowledge of the child?	How did I use that knowledge to inform instruction?	How did I teach in culturally relevant ways? What else might I do?	What specific skills, strategies, and dispositions are the children learning?	What standards are addressed?

FIGURE 6.1: Questions to help you chart your own practice.

grade-level groups to discuss those moments and connect them to specific principles, beliefs, and standards.

What are some other formats/venues for professional reflection?

While the learning community format suggested in this section is an excellent structure for professional study, there are numerous other ways that teachers and administrators can join together for focused reflection. Some of the examples presented below represent further possibilities for long-term study. Others are shared as possibilities for supplementing ongoing study with shorter-term experiences.

Book clubs. Members read and discuss books. This could include professional literature as well as children's books. Tips for starting a Teachers as Readers Book Group can be found at www.ncte.org/positions/statements/teachersasreaders.

Grade-level meetings. Grade-level meetings can be great places for focused reflection and study. In some schools, this will mean rethinking current views about grade-level meetings. When these spaces focus primarily on replicating curriculum from room to room—planning for teaching the same thing at the same time in the same way—there is no support for teachers to draw on their own styles and embrace the strengths and needs of their own students. While there are certainly some key understandings, skills, dispositions, and abilities important to cultivate at each grade level, grade-level meetings are most effective when teachers engage in professional study and reflection that supports growth while celebrating autonomous decisions in individual classrooms.

National, state, and local conferences. Attending professional conferences is a fabulous way for teachers to access resources and support for focused reflection. Through these experiences, teachers share their work and learn from others in ways that will ultimately enhance successful teaching in their home districts and schools. Administrators and policymakers can make a huge difference in the vitality of their schools and districts by making travel to conferences possible. Sadly, there has been a recent move in many districts and states to shut down out-of-state travel, but this is a matter of priority. It is not impossible to reconsider the allocation of funds to provide funding for conference travel. Another idea is to create a grants base within district offices and schools, hiring persons with expertise in obtaining large-scale grants to support teachers' opportunities to become intellectually rein-vigorated by engaging with colleagues from across the country.

Graduate course work. Often teachers enroll in graduate courses or degree programs as a way to engage in focused, professional reflec-tion. Graduate course work can provide access to a range of current and respected texts and ideas in the field that educators can use to support more localized learning in school-based study groups and book clubs.

Online forums. Online forums are another space for reflection and growth. Participating in such forums, teachers gain insights from across the country as they have opportunities to share their work and learn from others' classrooms. With other teachers, they address challenges, pose questions, provide insight, and find new ideas about practice, materials, and other resources. One space to do this is by participating in NCTE's connected community (www.ncte.org). Also, www.readwritethink.org provides an interactive place to find innovative lesson plans and to con-tribute some of your own.

Planning for Teaching

The ultimate purpose of focused reflection is to inform classroom instruction and affect student learning. In this section, we provide suggestions to support the move from reflection to planning. We think about this in terms of large-scale (overall structures, unit planning, student inquiries) and small-scale (meeting the needs of individual children) planning. These suggestions are shared as one way to use ideas presented in this book as you continue to plan for your own classroom. Figure 6.2 incorporates ideas and issues from all sections of the book to offer a big-picture overview—foundations to consider as you plan.

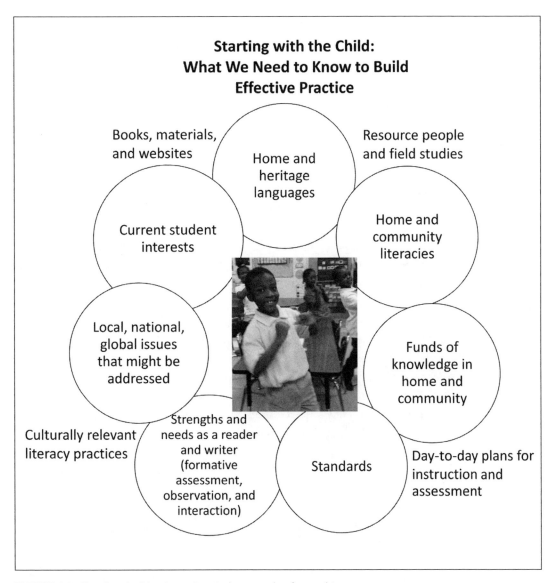

FIGURE 6.2: Keeping the big picture in mind as you plan for teaching.

Preparing to Plan: Keeping Students at the Center

You are engaged in reflective experiences within and beyond your professional community. You read research and examine accounts of other teachers at work. You recognize that teacher knowledge is foundational to making wise choices in classrooms. You look to standards as one resource in that process. So, it's time to take stock, to consider what you know and what you need to know about your students, so you can keep them at the center as you plan.

Keeping the students at the center means figuring out what students know and then making decisions about how to move them forward. Also, knowledge of each student is the primary lens through which to interpret and implement standards of any kind. Effective large-scale and small-scale planning can only be developed when teachers know their students well. A first step in knowing your students is the obvious one—making spaces during the school day to listen carefully and interact purposefully.

Examples of making space for careful listening are evidenced throughout the Section II vignettes. Mariel, an exceptional listener, pays close attention to children as they work. She asks the right questions at the right time to elicit responses that inform her next moves. As a result, she is able to effectively support students as writers. Julia learned about her students by spending time with them *and* their families, giving her deeper understandings about the issues they faced and the knowledge they possessed. As a result, she was able to accurately predict that she could engage her students as readers if she brought in books that supported talk about the immigration issues that were so meaningful to them. Mary built curriculum about the manufacture of clothing because she set up opportunities for student interaction and listened to discover what would motivate and educate her students. And, Nancy Boggs sent home cameras and used the photos to prompt students' poetry about people and events important in their lives. In the process, she learned about families and their knowledge as well as the specific literacy needs of her students.

As these teachers got to know their students, they were also able to listen to them with an ear for local, national, and global issues that would motivate and challenge their learners. As a result, they created opportunities to support students in learning to think critically. At the same time, they taught specific literacy skills and addressed standards. Because they made spaces to listen to and interact with their students and families in and out of school, these teachers were able to identify students' interests, expertise, and needs and plan for instruction. The questions in Figure 6.3 are provided to help you think in the same way as you prepare for instruction.

Reflexive Planning Questions*	Notes
What do I know about:	
• My students' home and heritage languages?	
• Funds of knowledge in my students' homes and communities?	
• Literacies that my students and their families use in homes and communities and could contribute to classroom learning?	
• Students' current interests?	
• Each student, as a reader and a writer (determined through daily interaction, observation, and formative assessment)?	
What are local, national, global needs/issues this study might address? (How might I help my students think critically through this unit of study?)	
What standards need to be addressed at this point? Generically (for the whole class) and for groups of children and individuals?	

*These questions are derived from documents developed through the collaborative work of Early Childhood faculty at the University of South Carolina: Gloria Boutte, Saudah Collins, Erin Miller, and Beth Powers-Costello.

FIGURE 6.3: Reflexive questions to help guide your planning and instruction.

What Do We Do with This Knowledge?

Planning Units of Study

A wide range of fabulous professional texts provide support for teachers as they use the kinds of questions posed above to plan units of study/inquiry. Again, examples of this kind of teaching are evident in the Section II vignettes. Freida engaged her students in a long-term inquiry about caterpillars and butterflies because of their fascination with the insects that frequented their schoolyard. Janice and Carmen involved students in collecting oral histories in their local

> **Resources to Support Inquiry-Based Teaching**
>
> "African American Communities: Implications for Culturally Relevant Teaching" (Boutte & Hill, 2006)
>
> *Black Ants and Buddhists: Thinking Critically and Teaching Differently in the Primary Grades* (Cowhey, 2006)
>
> *Children's Language: Connecting Reading, Writing, and Talk* (Lindfors, 2008)
>
> *Inquiry at the Window: Pursuing the Wonders of Learners* (Whitin & Whitin, 1997)
>
> *Learning Together through Inquiry: From Columbus to Integrated Curriculum* (Short et al., 1996)
>
> *Looking Closely and Listening Carefully: Learning Literacy through Inquiry* (Mills, O'Keefe, & Jennings, 2004)

community and used students' music to build from their worlds while promoting appreciation for community heritage. Julia's second-grade literature discussions about issues of immigration built curriculum from realities in the lives of the children.

While engaging students in these ways, the vignette teachers addressed all of the skills, strategies, and content in their district pacing guides and state standards. Freida knew that it was important for her students to learn about scientific inquiry and how to represent information in written text, so, as the children learned about insects and butterflies, she structured mini-lessons and 1–1 conferences to be sure they understood the scientific process and strategies for writing nonfiction texts. Janice and Carmen knew that the first-grade curriculum included a focus on community as well as on developing knowledge of high-frequency words and word patterns. To address those standards, they highlighted content about communities and practiced high-frequency words and word patterns in the context of the oral history experience. While these teachers paid careful attention to district and state requirements, the pathways they used to teach content, skills, and strategies were significantly unique to the learners in their classrooms.

In the same ways, you can think about your knowledge of *your* students (based on the Reflexive Planning Questions in Figure 6.3), and use that knowledge to design units of study/inquiry. We provide a structure in Figure 6.4 that draws on your answers to those reflexive questions to help you organize unit, theme, or inquiry plans.

Day-to-Day Planning

Once a unit plan is developed, it's time to bring specificity to the plan by figuring out how your ideas will be integrated within the structure of your school day. The planning chart in Figure 6.5 provides one way to look at that level of planning. Our intent is not that this chart become a required format for teachers' weekly planning, but that it will be used to help teachers and administrators think together about ways that thoughtful teaching might look across a school day. The daily schedule that we have outlined here, the curricular elements within it, and the sequence in which those elements are presented constitute one of many possible structures.

It is beyond the scope of this book to present strategies for *how* to teach specific skills and strategies during each component of the school day. However, educators can access a wide range of excellent texts that provide that kind of specificity—thoughtful strategies

---

Recommended Professional Books: Teaching Strategies

Becoming Writers in the Elementary Classroom: Visions and Decisions (Van Sluys, 2011)

Choice Words: How Our Language Affects Children's Learning (Johnston, 2004)

How's It Going? A Practical Guide to Conferring with Student Writers (Anderson, 2000)

Literacy Achievement and Diversity: Keys to Success for Students, Teachers, and Schools (Au, 2011)

Literacy in the Welcoming Classroom: Creating Family-School Partnerships That Support Student Learning (Allen, 2010)

Literate Lives: Teaching Reading and Writing in Elementary Classrooms (Flint, 2008)

Study Driven: A Framework for Planning Units of Study in the Writing Workshop (Ray, 2006)

Time for Literacy Centers: How to Organize and Differentiate Instruction (Owocki, 2005)

Using Reflexive Questions to Plan*	
Based on my responses to the Reflexive Planning Questions, the topic for our upcoming inquiry/unit of study will be:	
Materials and books I need to gather to support this inquiry/unit of study:	
Ways this study will be culturally responsive and relevant to my students:	
Ways this study will embrace the home languages of my students:	
Ways this study will broaden my students' cultural and linguistic worlds:	
People I will call on as resources, websites, and/or field studies (excursions outside school):	
Ways this unit of study will help my students think critically and work toward making a difference:	
Organizational ideas for my room/walls to support this inquiry/unit of study:	
Standards this unit of study will address:	

*This chart is derived from documents developed through the collaborative work of Early Childhood faculty at the University of South Carolina: Gloria Boutte, Saudah Collins, Erin Miller, and Beth Powers-Costello.

FIGURE 6.4: Chart to help you use reflexive questions to plan.

for meeting students' needs during shared reading, mini-lessons, reading and writing conferences, small-group work, centers, and so on. We suggest that teachers and administrators explore these kinds of texts within their professional learning communities to find further support for addressing the needs of every child.

Trying Out New Ideas

The structures provided in the first section of this chapter suggest that teachers try out new teaching strategies in their classrooms and then discuss them during meetings of their professional learning communities. It is worth mentioning again that it will be easier and more effective (and more fun) if you have at least one partner (from a neighboring classroom or another school) who is trying out similar ideas and/or trying to meet similar goals. As you and your colleagues try out new strategies in your respective classrooms, you can evaluate them together using the learning goals you have established: Discuss what you are trying to accomplish and how well you are meeting those goals. Then work together to tweak the ideas and try again. You might

Planning Each Day: One Possibility					
How will I use the information from Reflexive Unit Planning to plan day-to-day?					
Topic of Inquiry/Unit Focus _____					
Teaching/Learning Structure	**Focus for Today**	**Books and Materials Needed**	**Standard(s) Addressed**	**How will I assess learning?**	**Where do we go next?**
Settling in Time					
Morning Gathering Time (songs, read-alouds, morning message; could also be a time for a science or social studies content lesson about the unit/inquiry topic; and classroom visitors/resources)					
Interactive Writing					
Writing Workshop • Mini-lesson (and validating yesterday's lessons)					
• 1–1 Conferences					
• Whole-Group Sharing (individual students share from today's work: writing strategies used, well-crafted phrases, newly used vocabulary, expressive language, etc.)					
Shared Reading					
Independent Reading • Mini-lesson (and validating yesterday's lesson)					
• 1–1 Reading Conferences					
• Whole-Group Sharing (individual students share based on their reading today: reading strategies, content learning, authors' craft, new vocabulary encountered)					
Literacy Invitations/Centers/Investigation Areas					
• Small-Group Reading Strategy Work					
• Literature Discussion Groups					
Whole-Class Validation of Learning (capturing and affirming learning from the day)					

FIGURE 6.5: Daily planning chart.

then want to share your results with your grade-level group or professional learning community.

A terrific example of just such a partnership is the story told by two kindergarten teachers, Donna Bell and Donna Jarvis, who worked together to transform their classrooms (Bell & Jarvis, 2002). They planned together, tried out new practices according to their own styles, and came together every few days to reflect, discuss, and revise. Their support for each other meant that, when an idea did not go as anticipated in one classroom, the experiences of the other teacher often provided insights helpful in making changes that led to success. Key to success, however, was the autonomy they felt in being able to accept or reject ideas based on what would work for the students in *their* classrooms and their individual teaching styles.

Share Ideas Online with Colleagues Near and Far

As you plan, collaborate with colleagues, learn, and teach, we hope you will share your ideas through NCTE's Connected Community or other online forums for teachers. All of the figures and charts found in this book are available for your use and adaptation on the Connected Community site. As you access them (or the interactive lesson plans at www.readwritethink.org), take a few moments to share your thinking related to teaching and planning—successes, challenges, solutions, epiphanies. Supporting each other online is one more way to strengthen our ability to help every student succeed and to remind ourselves that colleagues nationwide are negotiating similar challenges, but also experiencing similar joys. In a profession where we all largely perform the obligations and duties of our role as teachers alone in our classrooms, it is critically important to remember that you are not alone.

Engaging as Advocates

Throughout this chapter we have discussed ways in which you can work to make sense of, put into perspective, and act in relation to the new standards without compromising your visions of great teaching. In this final section we invite you to consider how you—teachers and administrators—can advocate for support that will enable you to sustain and enhance the innovative spirit and knowledge that leads to classroom excellence.

The vignette teachers in Section II highlight powerful ways of shaping instruction based on strong convictions about teaching and learning. They create pathways to learning that are unique to their classrooms, yet consistent with each other, because of those common convictions. They address standards by starting with the child and focusing on preparing students to contribute to a world we can only imagine today. An important aspect of this strength and expertise is the teachers' ability to advocate—on their own and in collaboration with others near and far—for their own professional needs and therefore their students' learning needs. In the following pages, we build on earlier conversations to suggest topics and strategies in support of your own educational advocacy.

As you reflect on these advocacy suggestions, keep in mind that specificity is an important element in helping others understand issues that concern you. Whether you are making a case for thoughtful teaching in grade-level or school board meetings, with parents, administrators, or in a legislator's office, your efforts will be greatly enhanced when you can share real stories about real children. The more you demonstrate the success of your efforts in explicit ways, the more successful your advocacy efforts will be. With that in mind, we share the following ideas that may be helpful as you advocate for students, teaching, and the profession.

Advocate for teachers' autonomy as instructional and curricular decision makers by participating in consistent, ongoing professional study.

Every teacher knows that professional autonomy is not a given, but when autonomy is paired with teachers' and administrators' commitment to participation in and support of professional study, possibilities for excellence grow exponentially. As demonstrated throughout this book, thoughtful teaching *is* possible in a time of standards if "talented teachers who care most deeply about their students" (Nieto, 2003, p. 9) are given the support to teach in inspirational ways. Thus, when considering the Common Core State Standards, it is important to interrupt tendencies to use them as a means to homogenize teaching: to create inflexible classroom schedules, cloned instructional units, and scripted lessons that take away teachers' unique styles and ability to address individual students' needs. To make this happen, administrators and teachers need to work together to create cultures of intellect in their schools and districts. Everyone needs to speak up to make consistent programs of ongoing professional study a reality.

Advocate for your expertise in developing and using assessment that informs instruction.

The importance of formative assessment as the cornerstone of what is currently being described as data-driven instruction has been discussed and demonstrated throughout this book. You know the local needs of your students and the community that supports their learning in and out of school. Therefore, you and your colleagues are best suited to design, implement, and adjust the formative assessments that will best enable you to meet your students' needs and, at the same time, address standards.

Advocating for this kind of assessment means sharing what you do with administrators, family members, and legislators. Keep a digital camera close at hand and document children's work and your 1–1, small-group, and whole-group moments with them. Document ways that you learn about each child as a reader and writer and how you use that documentation to make decisions that move each child forward. Make students' progress visible. Use those documents to share the information you obtain through formative assessments and the impact of that information on instruction and student learning in contrast to the limitations of high-stakes tests.

Advocate for assessments that capture students' knowledge, including their expertise in negotiating within and across languages and cultural traditions.

As you advocate for formative assessments, insist on using assessment materials that are culturally and linguistically relevant—materials to which *your* students can relate. Explain to administrators, family members, and policymakers that when you assess in languages and with materials that are not relevant to students, you cannot get an accurate read on what they know and can do. To help you acquire and create linguistically and culturally appropriate assessments, access family members and language experts in your communities, as well as the resources provided in Section I of this book.

Advocate for the appropriate *use* of assessments.

Nieto (2003) writes with a concern voiced by many teachers: "At times it seems that teachers' work is valued only for its conspicuous conformity to standards-based accountability plans and test performance" (p. 2). Advocate against the use of assessments to grade schools and assign merit pay for teachers. Such policies are counterproductive to creating cultures of intellect that lead to success for all students in school. Teachers and administrators can redirect the use of assessment to the place it belongs—informing instructional decisions made for students day-to-day. For this to happen, the stand you take must be taken together.

Advocate for student learning by designing instruction and selecting materials based on your knowledge of *your* students.

Rigid interpretations of standards often lead to the imposition of programs that tell teachers what to do and say and the materials they must use. These scripted programs limit what teachers can do in support of student learning because they prevent educators from drawing on professional knowledge and knowledge of each child to design instruction and select materials. Scripts do not know children and their communities. Teachers do.

Administrators and policymakers: Work within your schools and districts to advocate for policies that support teachers' right to make decisions about instruction and materials. Remember that the CCSS do not advocate for a particular literacy pedagogy, program, or set of materials. In fact, it is made clear in the standards materials that *teachers* are the decision makers for their classrooms.

Advocate for teaching that supports all students as purposeful, proficient, and critical consumers and producers of literacies.

High-stakes tests often born of standards movements can also lead to narrow views of knowledge and instruction, consequently limiting possibilities for teaching and learning. Too often, in the name of test prep, curriculum becomes focused on skills taught in isolation rather than skill-teaching in the context of opportunities to create, consume, and analyze real-world texts with purpose, passion, and proficiency. This is of concern for all students but particularly for those who, because of low test scores, are relegated to a steady diet of uninspiring curriculum and instruction, "leaving [them] with the least access to the kind of learning that will prepare them for college and contemporary careers" (Darling-Hammond, 2010, p. 72). This is a serious inequity that needs to be addressed by educators and community members advocating together. So while we advocate for better assessments and better use of assessments, we must also advocate for teaching that moves students far beyond the narrow parameters of test prep. We know that, in the current climate, high test scores provide access to education, jobs, and other opportunities, so we have the responsibility to prepare every student to master the testing genre. But we cannot confuse test preparation with helping students develop the expertise, insight, and knowledge necessary to contribute to and succeed within and across worlds beyond the classroom.

Advocate for inclusive definitions of language and literacies and culturally relevant practices.

Like Genishi and Dyson (2009), we have no objection to students "working toward reasonable goals" (p. 32), but those goals must be designed to appreciate a rich "multiplicity of language and language varieties" (p. 33). It is the same with appreciating the rich cultural histories of families and communities, as well as family orientations and beliefs. Use your knowledge of culturally relevant teaching and its benefits to advocate for embracing the cultural heritages, orientations, languages, and belief systems in your classroom. To support your advocacy, draw on evidence (through existing research and your own practice) about ways that this kind of teaching increases the learning potential for all students. Seek, find, celebrate, and utilize the languages and literacies that exist in the homes and communities of your students as well as in the broader local and global communities. Fill your classroom and the halls of your schools with wide varieties of languages, literacies, communities, and family structures. Move from a tourist approach to helping children get to know people, community practices, and issues.

Advocate for yourself and your students by contributing to larger professional communities.

The onslaught of attacks against teachers by those who question our professional knowledge is frustrating and demoralizing. Connecting with others to give voice to your expertise is one amazingly powerful way to begin speaking back persuasively. Although educators' days are consumed by the immediate needs of students, families, and colleagues and it can feel overwhelming to think of joining larger professional organizations, the time and energy necessary to do so are well worth it and less extensive than you might think. You do have a lot to share; just as you benefit from hearing other teachers' stories, they will benefit from yours. Professional organizations (their conferences, websites, and chat rooms) such as the National Council of Teachers of English (http://www.ncte.org), the National Association for the Education of Young Children (http://www.naeyc.org), the International Reading Association (http://www.reading.org), the National Association for Bilingual Education (http://www.nabe.org), and the National Association for Multicultural Education (http://www.nameorg.org)—to name a few—can be spaces where you can find renewal, solace, and empowerment. In this time of the Common Core State Standards, we believe that the work illustrated by the vignette teachers and similarly enacted by teachers like you can be leveraged toward powerful ends. By connecting with each other locally, nationally, and internationally, we have the power to influence our students, each other, and the teaching profession.

Finally . . .

My whole philosophy of teaching can be summed up as: *Follow the child.* Over the years, it's become clear to me that I can guide children in learning skills by relating those skills to their interests. I bring this same approach to the way that I incorporate state standards in my teaching. I ask questions such as, What does this child need in order to progress? Which standards will help me focus on those needs? Which standards are most important for my students? In this way, I use the children's needs to prioritize my approach to the standards. As a result, I am able to coordinate the standards with the activities going on in the classroom with relative ease. And, perhaps more important, I am able to accomplish this without losing focus on what matters most—my students.
—*Freida Hammett, Grades 1–3*

Throughout this book, we have tried to illustrate links between educators' innovative spirit, knowledge, and visions and the ease with which standards can be addressed without compromising those visions. Readers will have many more ideas for accomplishing the same goals. As we work together toward these goals, we continue to raise the bar by supporting the growth of "reflective, moral, and active citizens [who have] the knowledge, skills, and commitment" to contribute to an interconnected world (Banks, 2007, p. 153)—our ultimate purpose as literacy educators. With that in mind, we close by inviting you—teachers, administrators, and policymakers—to support educational policies and practices that make a difference. We urge you to connect with one another as you advocate for excellence, equity, and innovation in educational institutions. In doing so, we can all support the work of inspirational teachers in the lives of children.

Appendix A

Resources

Following is a consolidation of the professional resources provided throughout this text, with the addition of a few others. They are shared to provide support for educators' ongoing discussions, study groups, and individual inquiries within professional learning communities in a time of Common Core State Standards—or anytime.

Topic	Resource
Teachers as learners: Resources for professional learning communities	Bell, D., & Jarvis, D. (2002). Letting go of "letter of the week." *Primary Voices, 11*(2), 10–24.
	Cahnmann-Taylor, M., & Souto-Manning, M. (2010). *Teachers act up! Creating multicultural learning communities through theatre*. New York: Teachers College Press.
	Cochran-Smith, M., & Lytle, S. L. (2009*). Inquiry as stance: Practitioner researcher for the next generation*. New York: Teachers College Press.
	Cody, A. (2011, May 2). Here's to the teachers! Retrieved from http://www.saveourschoolsmarch.org/2011/05/02/heres-to-the-teachers/
	Darling-Hammond, L. (1997). *The right to learn: A blueprint for creating schools that work*. San Francisco: Jossey Bass.
	Darling-Hammond, L., & Bransford, J. (with LePage, D., Hammerness, K., & Duffy, H.). (Eds.). (2005). *Preparing teachers for a changing world: What teachers should learn and be able to do*. San Francisco: Jossey Bass.
	Donnelly, A., Morgan, D. N., DeFord, D. E., Files, J., Long, S., & Mills, H. (2005). Transformative professional development: Negotiating knowledge with an inquiry stance. *Language Arts, 82*(5), 336–46.
	Fecho, B. (2011). *Teaching for the students: Habits of heart, mind, and practice in the engaged classroom*. New York: Teachers College Press.
	Hankins, K. H. (2003). *Teaching through the storm: A journal of hope*. New York: Teachers College Press.
	Lieberman, A., & Miller, L. (Eds.). (2008). *Teachers in professional communities: Improving teaching and learning*. New York: Teachers College Press.
	Long, S., Abramson, A., Boone, A., Borchelt, C., Kalish, R., Miller, E., Parks, J., & Tisdale, C. (2006). *Tensions and triumphs in the early years of teaching: Real-world findings and advice for supporting new teachers*. Urbana, IL: National Council of Teachers of English.

Topic	Resource
Teachers as learners: Resources for professional learning communities (continued)	Meier, D. (2002). *In schools we trust: Creating communities of learning in an era of testing and standardization*. Boston: Beacon Press.
	Mills, H., & Donnelly, A. (2001). *From the ground up: Creating a culture of inquiry*. Portsmouth, NH: Heinemann.
	Nieto, S. (2003). *What keeps teachers going?* New York: Teachers College Press.
	Nieto, S. (Ed.). (2005). *Why we teach*. New York: Teachers College Press.
	Perry, T., Moses, R. P., Wynne, J. T., Cortés, E., Jr., & Delpit, L. (Eds.). (2010). *Quality education as a constitutional right: Creating a grassroots movement to transform public schools*. Boston: Beacon Press.
	Strickland, D. S., & Riley-Ayers, S. (2007). *Literacy leadership in early childhood: The essential guide*. New York: Teachers College Press.
Resources for selecting children's books	Bishop, R. S. (2007). *Free within ourselves: The development of African American children's literature*. Portsmouth, NH: Heinemann.
	Circle of Inclusion. (2002). *Nine ways to evaluate children's books that address disability as part of diversity*. Retrieved from http://www.circleofinclusion.org/english/books/section1/a.html
	Fox, D. L., & Short, K. G. (Eds.). (2003). *Stories matter: The complexity of cultural authenticity in children's literature*. Urbana, IL: National Council of Teachers of English.
	Fresch, M. J. (1995). Self-selection of early literacy learners. *The Reading Teacher, 49*(3), 220–27.
	Galda, L., Cullinan, B. E., & Sipe, L. R. (2010). *Literature and the child* (7th ed.). Belmont, CA: Wadsworth-Cengage Learning.
	Horn Book. (2011). *The Horn Book: Publications about books for children and young adults*. Retrieved from http://www.hbook.com/
	In Time. (n.d.) *Evaluating children's books for bias*. Retrieved from http://www.intime.uni.edu/multiculture/curriculum/children.htm
	Lehman, B. A., Freeman, E. B., & Scharer, P. L. (2010). *Reading globally, K–8: Connecting students to the world through literature*. Thousand Oaks, CA: Corwin Press.
	Peterson, B. (2001). *Literary pathways: Selecting books to support new readers*. Portsmouth, NH: Heinemann.
	Ringgold, Faith. [Website of artist and writer, Faith Ringgold]. http://www.faithringgold.com/
	Short, K. G. (1997). *Literature as a way of knowing*. York, ME: Stenhouse.
	Short, K. G., & Pierce, K. M. (1998). *Talking about books: Literature discussion groups in K–8 classrooms*. Portsmouth, NH: Heinemann.
	Sipe, L. R., & Pantaleo, S. (Eds.). (2008). *Postmodern picturebooks: Play, parody, and self-referentiality*. New York: Routledge.
	Szymusiak, K., Sibberson, F., & Koch, L. (2008). *Beyond leveled books: Supporting early and transitional readers in grades K–5* (2nd ed.). Portland, ME: Stenhouse.
Selecting and using nonfiction books with children	Dorfman, L. R., & Cappelli, R. (2009). *Nonfiction mentor texts: Teaching informational writing through children's literature, K–8*. Portland, ME: Stenhouse.
	Heard, G., & McDonough, J. (2009). *A place for wonder: Reading and writing nonfiction in the primary grades*. Portland, ME: Stenhouse.
	Portalupi, J., & Fletcher, R. (2001). *Nonfiction craft lessons: Teaching information writing K–8*. Portland, ME: Stenhouse.
	Stead, T. (2001). *Is that a fact? Teaching nonfiction writing K–3*. Portland, ME: Stenhouse.

Topic	Resource
Families and communities as resources	Allen, J. (2007). *Creating welcoming schools: A practical guide to home-school partnerships with diverse families.* New York: Teachers College Press.
	Dantas, M. L., & Manyak, P. C. (Eds.). (2009). *Home-school connections in a multicultural society: Learning from and with culturally and linguistically diverse families.* New York: Routledge.
	Dyson, A. H. (2003). *The brothers and sisters learn to write: Popular literacies in childhood and school cultures.* New York: Teachers College Press.
	Edwards, P. A. (2009). *Tapping the potential of parents: A strategic guide to boosting student achievement through family involvement.* New York: Scholastic.
	González, N., Moll, L. C., & Amanti, C. (Eds.). (2005). *Funds of knowledge: Theorizing practices in households, communities, and classrooms.* New York: Erlbaum.
	Gregory, E., Long, S., & Volk, D. (Eds.). (2004). *Many pathways to literacy: Young children learning with siblings, grandparents, peers and communities.* New York: Routledge.
	Kinloch, V. (2010). *Harlem on our minds: Place, race and the literacies of urban youth.* New York: Teachers College Press.
	Kyle, D. W., McIntyre, E., Miller, K. B., & Moore, G. H. (2002). *Reaching out: A K–8 resource for connecting families and schools.* Thousand Oaks, CA: Corwin Press.
	López-Robertson, J., Long, S., & Turner-Nash, K. (2010). First steps in constructing counter narratives of young children and their families. *Language Arts, 88*(2), 93–103.
	Marsh, M. M., & Turner-Vorbeck, T. (Eds.). (2010). *(Mis)understanding families: Learning from real families in our schools.* New York: Teachers College Press.
	Pahl, K., & Rowsell, J. (2010). *Artifactual literacies: Every object tells a story.* New York: Teachers College Press.
	Taylor, D. (1997). *Many families, many literacies: An international declaration of principles.* Portsmouth, NH: Heinemann.
Supporting bilingualism/ multilingualism	Edelsky, C., Smith, K., & Faltis, C. (2008). *Side by side learning: Exemplary literacy practices for English language learners and English speakers in the mainstream classroom.* New York: Scholastic.
	Fassler, R. (2003). *Room for talk: Teaching and learning in a multilingual kindergarten.* New York: Teachers College Press.
	Freeman, D. E., & Freeman, Y. S. (2011). *Between worlds: Access to second language acquisition* (3rd ed.). Portsmouth, NH: Heinemann.
	Fu, D. (2009). *Writing between languages: How English language learners make the transition to fluency, grades 4–12.* Portsmouth, NH: Heinemann.
	García, O., & Kleifgen, J. A. (2010). *Educating emergent bilinguals: Policies, programs, and practices for English language learners.* New York: Teachers College Press.
	Genishi, C., & Dyson, A. H. (2009). *Children, language, and literacy: Diverse learners in diverse times.* New York: Teachers College Press.
	Jarmal, M., & Schneider, K. (2005). *Speaking in tongues: Four kids, four languages, one city, one world* [film]. San Francisco: PatchWorks Films. Retrieved from http://speakingintonguesfilm.info/
	Krashen, S. D. (2003). *Explorations in language acquisition and use.* Portsmouth, NH: Heinemann.
	Menken, K., & García, O. (Eds.). (2010). *Negotiating language policies in schools: Educators as policymakers.* New York: Routledge.
	Reyes, M., de la Luz (Ed.). (2011). *Words were all we had: Becoming biliterate against the odds.* New York: Teachers College Press.

Topic	Resource
Supporting bilingualism/ multilingualism *(continued)*	Scott, J. C., Straker, D. Y., & Katz, L. (Eds.). (2009). *Affirming students' right to their own language: Bridging language policies and pedagogical practices.* New York: Routledge.
	Teachers of English to Speakers of Other Languages (TESOL). http://www.tesol.org
	Valdés, G., Capitelli, S., & Alvarez, L. (2011). *Latino children learning English: Steps in the journey.* New York: Teachers College Press.
	Van Sluys, K. (2005). *What if and why? Literacy invitations for multilingual classrooms.* Portsmouth, NH: Heinemann.
Selecting books to support emerging bilingual students	Brown, Monica. *Monica Brown: Children's book author.* http://www.monicabrown.net/
	Cinco Puntos. http://www.cincopuntos.com/
	Mora, Pat. *Bookjoy: Pat Mora: Author, presenter, literacy advocate.* http://www.patmora.com/
	Morales, Y. [Website of author and illustrator, Yuyi Morales]. http://www.yuyimorales.com/
	National Association for Bilingual Education (NABE). http://www.nabe.org
	National Association for Multicultural Education (NAME). http://www.nameorg.org/
African American language	Boutte, G. S. (2007). Teaching students who speak African American language (AAL): Expanding educators' and students' linguistic repertoire. In M. E. Brisk (Ed.), *Language, culture, and community in teacher education* (pp. 47–70). New York: Routledge.
	Delpit, L., & Dowdy, J. K. (Eds.). (2008). *The skin that we speak: Thoughts on language and culture in the classroom.* New York: New Press.
	Delpit, L., & Perry, T. (1998). *The real Ebonics debate: Power, language, and the education of African-American children.* Boston: Beacon Press.
	Rickford, J. R., & Rickford, R. J. (2000). *Spoken soul: The story of Black English.* New York: Wiley.
	Smitherman, G. (2006). *Word from the mother: Language and African Americans.* New York: Routledge.
	Wheeler, R. S., & Swords, R. (2006). *Code-switching: Teaching standard English in urban classrooms.* Urbana, IL: National Council of Teachers of English.
Equity in education	Banks, J. A. (2007). *Educating citizens in a multicultural society* (2nd ed.). New York: Teachers College Press.
	Darling-Hammond, L. (2010). *The flat world and education: How America's commitment to equity will determine our future.* New York: Teachers College Press.
	Genishi, C., & Goodwin, A. L. (2008). *Diversities in early childhood education: Rethinking and doing.* New York: Routledge.
	Howard, T. C. (2010). *Why race and culture matter in schools: Closing the achievement gap in America's classrooms.* New York: Teachers College Press.
	Irvine, J. J. (2003). *Educating teachers for diversity: Seeing with a cultural eye.* New York: Teachers College Press.
	Nieto, S. (2010). *The light in their eyes: Creating multicultural learning communities* (10th anniversary ed.). New York: Teachers College Press.
	Pelo, A. (2008). *Rethinking early childhood education.* Milwaukee, WI: Rethinking Schools.
	Southern Poverty Law Center. *Teaching Tolerance* [magazine]. www.tolerance.org
	Tatum, B. D. (2008). *Can we talk about race? And other conversations in an era of school resegregation.* Boston: Beacon Press.
	Walker, V. S. (1996). *Their highest potential: An African American school community in the segregated south.* Chapel Hill: University of North Carolina Press.

Topic	Resource
Culturally relevant pedagogies	Boutte, G. S., & Hill E. L. (2006). African American communities: Implications for culturally relevant teaching. *New Educator, 2*(4), 311–29.
	Campano, G. (2007). *Immigrant students and literacy: Reading, writing, and remembering.* New York: Teachers College Press.
	Edwards, P. A., McMillon, G. T., & Turner, J. D. (2010). *Change is gonna come: Transforming literacy education for African American students.* New York: Teachers College Press.
	Gay, G. (2011). *Culturally responsive teaching: Theory, research and practice* (2nd ed.) New York: Teachers College Press.
	Ladson-Billings, G. (2009). *The dreamkeepers: Successful teachers of African American children* (2nd ed.). San Francisco: Jossey Bass.
	McIntyre, E., Hulan, N., & Layne, V. (2011). *Reading instruction for diverse classrooms: Research-based, culturally responsive practice.* New York: Guilford Press.
	McIntyre, E., Rosebery, A., & González, N. (Eds.). (2001). *Classroom diversity: Connecting curriculum to students' lives.* Portsmouth, NH: Heinemann.
	Sleeter, C. E., & Cornbleth, C. (Eds.). (2011). *Teaching with vision: Culturally responsive teaching in standards-based classrooms.* New York: Teachers College Press.
	Soulja Boy. (2010). Pretty boy swag. On *The DeAndre way* [CD]. Los Angeles, CA: Interscope Records.
	Villegas, A. M., & Lucas, T. (2002). *Educating culturally responsive teachers: A coherent approach.* Albany: State University of New York Press.
Special needs	Fu, D., & Shelton, N. R. (2007). Including students with special needs in a writing workshop. *Language Arts, 84*(4), 325–36.
	Garcia, A., & Chiki, F. (2010). Note from the editors. *School Talk, 15*(4), 1, 4.
	Klingner, J. K., Artiles, A. J., Kozleski, E., Harry, B., Zion, S., Tate, W., Durán, G. Z., & Riley, D. (2005). Addressing the disproportionate representation of culturally and linguistically diverse students in special education through culturally responsive educational systems. *Education Policy Analysis Archives, 13*(38), 1–40.
	Lesley, M. (2003). A pedagogy of control: Worksheets and the special needs child. *Language Arts, 80*(6), 444–52.
	National Association of Special Education Teachers (NASET). http://www.naset.org/
	Pardini, P. (2002). Special education: Promises and problems. *Rethinking schools, 16*(3).
	Schwarz, P. (2006). *From disability to possibility: The power of inclusive classrooms.* Portsmouth, NH: Heinemann.
Teaching strategies	Allen, J. (2010). *Literacy in the welcoming classroom: Creating family-school partnerships that support student learning.* New York: Teachers College Press.
	Anderson, C. (2000). *How's it going? A practical guide to conferring with student writers.* Portsmouth, NH: Heinemann.
	Au, K. (2011). *Literacy achievement and diversity: Keys to success for students, teachers, and schools.* New York: Teachers College Press.
	Flint, A. S. (2008). *Literate lives: Teaching reading and writing in elementary classrooms.* Hoboken, NJ: Wiley.
	Johnston, P. H. (2004). *Choice words: How our language affects children's learning.* Portland, ME: Stenhouse.

Topic	Resource
Teaching strategies *(continued)*	Jones, S., Clarke, L. W., & Enriquez, G. (2010). *The reading turnaround: A five part framework for differentiated instruction.* New York: Teachers College Press.
	Krashen, S. D. (2004). *The power of reading: Insights from the research.* Westport, CT: Libraries Unlimited.
	Optiz, M. F., & Ford, M. P. (2001). *Reaching readers: Flexible and innovative strategies for guided reading.* Portsmouth, NH: Heinemann.
	Owocki, G. (2005). *Time for literacy centers: How to organize and differentiate instruction.* Portsmouth, NH: Heinemann.
	Ray, K. W. (2006). *Study driven: A framework for planning units of study in the writing workshop.* Portsmouth, NH: Heinemann.
	Short, K. G., & Harste, J. C. (with Burke, C.). (1996). *Creating classrooms for authors and inquirers.* Portsmouth, NH: Heinemann.
	Van Sluys, K. (2011). *Becoming writers in the elementary classroom: Visions and decisions.* Urbana, IL: National Council of Teachers of English.
Critical literacies	Allen, J. (Ed.). (1999). *Class actions: Teaching for social justice in elementary and middle school.* New York: Teachers College Press.
	Bomer, R., & Bomer, K. (2001). *For a better world: Reading and writing for social action.* Portsmouth, NH: Heinemann.
	Christensen, L. (2009). *Teaching for joy and justice: Re-imagining the language arts classroom.* Milwaukee, WI: Rethinking Schools.
	Cowhey, M. (2006). *Black ants and Buddhists: Thinking critically and teaching differently in the primary grades.* Portland, ME: Stenhouse.
	Shannon, P. (2011). *Reading wide awake: Politics, pedagogies, and possibilities.* New York: Teachers College Press.
	Vasquez, V. (2004). *Negotiating critical literacies with young children.* New York: Erlbaum.
	Vasquez, V. (2010). *Getting beyond "I like the book": Creating space for critical literacy in K–6 classrooms* (2nd ed.). Newark, DE: International Reading Association.
Assessment	Basterra, M., del Rosario, Trumbull, E., & Solano-Flores, G. (Eds.). (2011). *Cultural validity in assessment: Addressing linguistic and cultural diversity.* New York: Routledge.
	Enciso, P., Katz, L., Kiefer, B. Z., Price-Dennis, D., & Wilson, M. (2009). Refocusing on assessment. *Language Arts, 86*(5), 339.
	Hamann, E. T. (2008). Standards vs. "standards" knowledge. In M. Pollock (Ed.), *Everyday antiracism: Getting real about race in school* (pp. 98–101). New York: New Press.
	Johnston, P. H. (1997). *Knowing literacy: Constructive literacy assessment.* Portland, ME: Stenhouse.
	Long, S., & Sibberson, F. (Eds.). (2005). Broadening visions of what counts: Assessment as knowing and being known. *School Talk, 11*(1).
	Mills, H. (2005). It's all about looking closely and listening carefully. *School Talk, 11*(1), 1–2.
	NAEYC. (2009). *Supplement on screening and assessment of young English-language learners.* Retrieved from http://www.naeyc.org/positionstatements/cape
	Owocki, G., & Goodman, Y. (2002). *Kidwatching: Documenting children's literacy development.* Portsmouth, NH: Heinemann.
	Samway, K. D., & McKeon, D. (2007). *Myths and realities: Best practices for English language learners* (2nd ed.). Portsmouth, NH: Heinemann.
	Stephens, D. (forthcoming). *The marriage of reading assessment and instruction: Stories from artful teachers.* Urbana, IL: National Council of Teachers of English.

Topic	Resource
Inquiry-based planning	Boutte, G. S., & Hill, E. L. (2006). African American communities: Implications for culturally relevant teaching. *New Educator, 2*(4), 311–29.
	Cowhey, M. (2006). *Black ants and Buddhists: Thinking critically and teaching differently in the primary grades.* Portland, ME: Stenhouse.
	Lindfors, J. W. (2008). *Children's language: Connecting reading, writing, and talk.* New York: Teachers College Press.
	Mills, H., O'Keefe, T., & Jennings, L. B. (2004). *Looking closely and listening carefully: Learning literacy through inquiry.* Urbana, IL: National Council of Teachers of English.
	Short, K. G., Schroeder, J., Laird, J., Kauffman, G., Ferguson, M. J., & Crawford, K. M. (1996). *Learning together through inquiry: From Columbus to integrated curriculum.* Portland, ME: Stenhouse.
	Whitin, P., & Whitin, D. J. (1997). *Inquiry at the window: Pursuing the wonders of learners.* Portsmouth, NH: Heinemann.
Play in support of learning	Cooper, P. M. (2009). *The classrooms all young children need: Lessons in teaching from Vivian Paley.* Chicago: University of Chicago Press.
	Lindfors, J. W. (2008). *Children's language: Connecting reading, writing, and talk.* New York: Teachers College Press.
	Meier, D., Engel, B. S., & Taylor, B. (2010). *Playing for keeps: Life and learning on a public school playground.* New York: Teachers College Press.
	Ohanian, S. (2002). *What happened to recess and why are our children struggling in kindergarten?* New York: McGraw-Hill.
	Owocki, G. (1999). *Literacy through play.* Portsmouth, NH: Heinemann.
	Paley, V. G. (2004). *A child's work: The importance of fantasy play.* Chicago: University of Chicago Press.

Appendix B

NCTE Principles

Throughout this book, there have been references to the NCTE principles that guide inspiring and effective teachers such as those featured in the vignettes. Drawn from research and based on classroom practices that foster student learning, these principles provide the foundation on which excellent teaching and enhanced student learning is built. This section includes explanations of NCTE principles about several areas of instruction—reading, writing, speaking and listening, and language—along with principles on formative assessment, teaching English language learners, 21st century literacies, and the role of teachers as decision makers in planning and implementing instruction. This last is the overarching principle under which all the others are clustered because it speaks to the heart of teacher work.

The principles in this appendix represent a compilation of work created and endorsed by NCTE, much of which can be found and is referenced on the NCTE website. As you think about ways to begin planning and shifting your instruction to align with the CCSS, use this document as a reference and resource, grounding your instruction, as well, in established, research-based NCTE principles. Each set of principles is organized into two categories: what NCTE knows about learners and learning, and what that knowledge means for teachers in the classroom.

NCTE Principles Regarding Teachers as Decision Makers

. . . .

A number of NCTE documents affirm the role of teachers as decision makers. Among the most recent are the 2005 "Features of Literacy Programs: A Decision-Making Matrix," produced by the Commission on Reading; the 2008 Resolution passed by the Board of Directors on Scripted Curricula; and the 2010 Resolution on Affirming the Role of Teachers and Students in Developing Curriculum.

Both the CCSS and NCTE agree that teachers' professional judgment and experience should shape the way that the goals inherent in the CCSS will be reached. Common agreement on what students should be able to accomplish leaves ample room for teachers to make decisions about the materials and strategies that will be used in the classroom. Teachers are not simply implementation agents for the CCSS; rather, they are active shapers of schoolwide plans that will enable students to reach the goals of these or any standards.

The journeys recounted in this book demonstrate that teachers work, learn, and plan most effectively when they collaborate with their colleagues. Indeed, research shows that teaching teams are a vital unit of school change and improvement.

What we know about teaching as a profession:

Working in teams allows teachers to design and share goals and strategies, strengthens the foundation for informed decision making, and contributes to participation in more broadly based communities of practice. Teaching teams bring together teachers, administrators, and other educators to:

- Develop and assess curricula
- Assess and become more knowledgeable about student learning
- Design and support activities that enhance professional practice
- Apply cross-disciplinary perspectives to curriculum design, assessment, and professional growth
- Conduct collective inquiry into the learning and teaching environment
- Connect to parents and the community

We also know that teaching is a professional endeavor, and that teachers are active problem solvers and decision makers in the classroom. As professionals, teachers and students benefit from sustained and empowering professional development for teachers.

What this means for educators:

- Administrators and teacher leaders should provide for systematic professional development as an essential component of successful school reform. Teachers who have opportunities for quality professional development are best able to help students learn.

- We need to collectively define teacher effectiveness as professional practice that uses deep content knowledge, effective pedagogy, authentic formative assessments, connections with parents and communities, sustained reflection, and research-based practices to engage students and help them learn.

- Schools should support a comprehensive literacy policy as described in the Literacy Education for All, Results for the Nation (LEARN) Act that requires a sustained investment in literacy learning and instruction from birth through grade 12 and empowers teachers to design and select formative assessments and lessons.

NCTE Principles Regarding Reading Instruction

The original version of this NCTE Guideline, titled "On Reading, Learning to Read, and Effective Reading Instruction: An Overview of What We Know and How We Know It," can be found on NCTE's website at http://www.ncte.org /positions/statements/onreading and was authored by The Commission on Reading of the National Council of Teachers of English.

As the teachers in this volume have demonstrated, reading instruction consumes a lot of our attention in the classroom. The creators of CCSS have acknowledged the importance of literacy for twenty-first-century learners by including standards for literacy instruction across content areas; indeed, as reading materials become more diverse and complex in this digital age, we need to prepare our students to encounter different types of texts in different situations.

What we know about reading and learning to read:

- Reading is a complex and purposeful sociocultural, cognitive, and linguistic process in which readers simultaneously use their knowledge of spoken and written language, their knowledge of the topic of the text, and their knowledge of their culture to construct meaning with text.
- Readers read for different purposes.
- As children learn to read continuous text, they use their intuitive knowledge of spoken language and their knowledge of the topic to figure out print words in text.
- The more children read, the better readers they become.
- Children read more when they have access to engaging, age-appropriate books, magazines, newspapers, computers, and other reading materials. They read more on topics that interest them than on topics that do not interest them.
- Reading supports writing development and writing supports reading development.
- All readers use their life experiences, their knowledge of the topic, and their knowledge of oral and written language to make sense of print.
- Readers continue to grow in their ability to make sense of an increasing variety of texts on an increasing variety of topics throughout their lives.

What this means for teachers of reading:

- Teachers should know their students as individuals, including their interests, their attitudes about reading, and their school, home, and community experiences.
- Teachers should read to students daily using a variety of text types.

- Teachers should try to use a variety of instructional groupings, including whole-group, small-group, and individual instruction, to provide multiple learning experiences.
- Teachers should teach before-, during-, and after-reading strategies for constructing meaning of written language, including demonstrations and think-alouds.
- Teachers should provide specific feedback to students to support their reading development.
- Teachers should provide regular opportunities for students to respond to reading through discussion, writing, art, drama, storytelling, music, and other creative expressions.
- Teachers should provide regular opportunities for students to reflect on their learning.
- Teachers should gradually release instructional responsibility to support independent reading.
- Teachers need to reflect on their students' progress and their own teaching practices to make changes that meet the needs of students.

NCTE Principles Regarding
the Teaching of Writing

The original version of this NCTE Guideline, titled "NCTE Beliefs about the Teaching of Writing," can be found on NCTE's website at http://www.ncte.org/positions/statements/writingbeliefs. It was originally authored by the Writing Study Group of the NCTE Executive Committee.

Just as the nature of and expectation for literacy has changed in the past century and a half, so has the nature of writing. Much of that change has been due to technological developments, from pen and paper, to typewriter, to word processor, to networked computer, to design software capable of composing words, images, and sounds. These developments not only expanded the types of texts that writers produce, but they also expanded immediate access to a wider variety of readers. The CCSS acknowledge this reality with standards that note the need for students to be able to use technology critically and effectively in their writing, but it is up to teachers to decide how to engage students with meaningful writing tasks that will enable them to meet the demands of our quickly changing society.

What we know about writing and learning to write:

- Everyone has the capacity to write, writing can be taught, and teachers can help students become better writers.
- People learn to write by writing.
- Writing is a process and a tool for thinking.
- Writing grows out of many different purposes.
- Conventions of finished and edited texts are important to readers and therefore to writers.
- Writing and reading are related.
- Literate practices are embedded in complicated social relationships.
- Composing occurs in different modalities and technologies.
- Assessment of writing involves complex, informed, human judgment.

What this means for teachers of writing:

- Writing instruction must include ample in-class and out-of-class opportunities for writing and should include writing for a variety of purposes and audiences.
- Instruction should be geared toward making sense in a life outside of school.
- Writing instruction must provide opportunities for students to identify the processes that work best for themselves as they move from one writing situation to another.
- Writing instruction must take into account that a good deal of workplace writing and other writing takes place in collaborative situations.
- It is important that teachers create opportunities for students to be in different kinds of writing situations, where the relationships and agendas are varied.
- Simply completing workbook or online exercises is inadequate.
- Students should have access to and experience in reading material that presents both published and student writing in various genres.
- Students should be taught the features of different genres experientially, not only explicitly.
- The teaching of writing should assume students will begin with the sort of language with which they are most at home and most fluent in their speech.
- Writing instruction must accommodate the explosion in technology from the world around us.
- Instructors must recognize the difference between formative and summative evaluation and be prepared to evaluate students' writing from both perspectives.

NCTE Principles Regarding
Speaking and Listening

NCTE principles on speaking and listening are articulated in "Guideline on the Essentials of English," which can be found at http://www.ncte.org/positions/statements/essentialsofenglish.

NCTE has a long history of supporting both instruction and assessment that integrates speaking and listening skills into the teaching of the English language arts, and the CCSS acknowledge the importance of speaking and listening in their Speaking and Listening Standards. Speaking refers to both informal speech such as talking in small groups or participating in class discussions and formal speech that results from composing and presenting a text. Listening means engaging in a complex active process that serves a variety of purposes.

What we know about speaking and listening in school:

- Public speaking is consistently ranked as one of the greatest sources of anxiety for people of all ages, and students are no exception.
- Much of the work of the classroom is done through speaking and listening.
- Formal speaking can be extemporaneous, relying on detailed notes but no actual script, or text-based.
- If students spend discussion time competing for the attention of the teacher rather than listening and responding to peers, they will not benefit from the informal speech in the classroom.
- It can be difficult to evaluate listening.
- One of the advantages of speaking is that it can generate immediate response, and it is important to make full use of this feature.

What this means for teachers of speaking and listening:

- To ensure that all students have an opportunity to develop skills of informal speech, teachers should not depend exclusively on volunteers in class discussion.
- Strategies for broadening participation include having all students respond in writing and then asking each student to respond aloud, asking students to discuss in pairs and report to the class, or distributing "talk tokens" that students can turn in after a contribution to a class discussion.

- Teachers should support the development of formal speaking and provide students with support and opportunities to practice so that they can feel well-prepared.
- Teachers need to give explicit attention to the connections between speaking and listening.
- To foster active listening, teachers can encourage students to build upon one another's contributions to discussions or require them to write a brief summary of the discussion at the end of class.

NCTE Principles Regarding Language Instruction

A comprehensive statement of NCTE's principles on language instruction appears in "Learning through Language: A Call for Action in All Disciplines," which can be found on NCTE's website at http://www.ncte.org/positions/statements/ learningthroughlang. It was prepared by NCTE's Language and Learning across the Curriculum Committee.

Language is a primary way individuals communicate what they think and feel. They find self-identity through language, shape their knowledge and experiences by means of it, and depend on it as a lifelong resource for expressing their hopes and feelings. One of the goals of language instruction is to foster language awareness among students so that they will understand how language varies in a range of social and cultural settings; how people's attitudes toward language vary across culture, class, gender, and generation; how oral and written language affects listeners and readers; how conventions in language use reflect social-political-economic values; how the structure of language works; and how first and second languages are acquired. The CCSS provide standards for language instruction, but teachers should use their knowledge of language to help foster an interest in language that is contextually bound to other literate practices.

What we know about language and learning language:

- As human beings, we can put sentences together even as children—we can all *do* grammar.

- Students make errors in the process of learning, and as they learn about writing, they often make new errors, not necessarily fewer ones.

- Students benefit much more from learning a few grammar keys thoroughly than from trying to remember many terms and rules.

- Students find grammar most interesting when they apply it to authentic texts.

- Inexperienced writers find it difficult to make changes in the sentences that they have written.

- All native speakers of a language have more grammar in their heads than any grammar book will ever contain.

What this means for teachers of language:

- Teachers should foster an understanding of grammar and usage.
- Instructors must integrate language study into all areas of the English language arts.
- Teachers should experiment with different approaches to language instruction until they find the ones that work the best for them and their students.
- Teachers should show students how to apply grammar not only to their writing but also to their reading and to their other language arts activities.
- Teachers can make good use of the other languages and the various dialects of English in their classrooms.
- Teachers might try using texts of different kinds, such as newspapers and the students' own writing, as sources for grammar examples and exercises.
- Teachers should use grammar exercises that improve writing, such as sentence combining and model sentences.

NCTE Principles Regarding Teaching English Language Learners

The original version of this NCTE Guideline, entitled "NCTE Position Paper on the Role of English Teachers in Educating English Language Learners (ELLs)," can be found on NCTE's website at http://www.ncte.org/positions/statements /teacherseducatingell. It was originally authored by members of the ELL Task Force: Maria Brisk, Stephen Cary, Ana Christina DaSilva Iddings, Yu Ren Dong, Kathy Escamilla, Maria Franquiz, David Freeman, Yvonne Freeman, Paul Kei Matsuda, Christina Ortmeier-Hooper, David Schwarzer, Katie Van Sluys, Randy Bomer (EC Liaison), and Shari Bradley (Staff Liaison).

Multilingual students differ in various ways, including level of oral English proficiency, literacy ability in both the heritage language and English, and cultural background. English language learners born in the United States often develop conversational language abilities in English but lack academic language proficiency. Newcomers, on the other hand, need to develop both conversational and academic English. The creators of CCSS note that the standards do not address the needs of English language learners (p. 6), but they also note that it is important for schools to consider and accommodate these students' needs while meeting the standards. These principles can provide a guide for teachers as they imagine what this might look like in their classrooms.

What we know about teaching multilingual learners:

- The academic language that students need in the different content areas differs.
- English language learners need three types of knowledge to become literate in a second language: the second language, literacy, and world knowledge.
- Second language acquisition is a gradual developmental process and is built on students' knowledge and skill in their native language.
- Bilingual students also need to learn to read and write effectively to succeed in school.
- Writing well in English is often the most difficult skill for English language learners to master.
- English language learners may not be familiar with terminology and routines often associated with writing instruction in the United States, including writing process, drafting, revision, editing, workshop, conference, audience, purpose, or genre.

What this means for teachers of multilingual students:

- For English language learners, teachers need to consider content objectives as well as English language development objectives.
- Because teachers relate to students both as learners and as children or adolescents, teachers must establish how they will address these two types of relationships, what they need to know about their students, and how they will acquire this knowledge.
- Teachers should provide authentic opportunities to use language in a nonthreatening environment.
- Teachers should encourage academic oral language in the various content areas.
- Teachers should give attention to the specific features of language students need to communicate in social as well as academic contexts.
- Teachers should include classroom reading materials that are culturally relevant.
- Teachers should ask families to read with students a version in the heritage language.
- Teachers should teach language features, such as text structure, vocabulary, and text- and sentence-level grammar, to facilitate comprehension of the text.
- Teachers should give students frequent meaningful opportunities for them to generate their own texts.
- Teachers should provide models of well-organized papers for the class.

NCTE Principles Regarding
21st Century Literacies

The original version of this Position Statement, titled "21st Century Curriculum and Assessment Framework," can be found on NCTE's website at http://www.ncte.org/positions/statements/21stcentframework. It was adopted by the NCTE executive committee on November 19, 2008.

Literacy has always been a collection of cultural and communicative practices shared among members of particular groups. These literacies—from reading online newspapers to participating in virtual classrooms—are multiple, dynamic, and malleable. Students need to be able to navigate the multiple literacy situations in which they will find themselves, and undoubtedly, they already engage with a number of literacies that were not available to their parents and teachers. The CCSS include standards for students' effective and critical use of technology, and the following principles can help teachers consider how to implement instruction that will empower students as technology continues to change and affect their literacies.

What we know about 21st century literacies and learning:

- As society and technology change, so does literacy.
- Because technology has increased the intensity and complexity of literate environments, the twenty-first century demands that a literate person possess a wide range of abilities and competencies, many literacies.
- Students in the twenty-first century need interpersonal skills to work collaboratively in both face-to-face and virtual environments to use and develop problem-solving skills.
- Students in the twenty-first century must be aware of the global nature of our world and be able to select, organize, and design information to be shared, understood, and distributed beyond their classrooms.
- Students in the twenty-first century must be able to take information from multiple places and in a variety of different formats, determine its reliability, and create new knowledge from that information.
- Students in the twenty-first century must be critical consumers and creators of multimedia texts.
- Students in the twenty-first century must understand and adhere to legal and ethical practices as they use resources and create information.

What this means for teachers of twenty-first-century learners:

- Students should use technology as a tool for communication, research, and creation of new works.
- Students should find relevant and reliable sources that meet their needs.
- Teachers should encourage students to take risks and try new things with tools available to them.
- Teachers should create situations and assignments in which students work in a group in ways that allow them to create new knowledge or to solve problems that can't be created or solved individually.
- Students should work in groups of members with diverse perspectives and areas of expertise.
- Students should be given opportunities to share and publish their work in a variety of ways.
- Teachers should help students analyze the credibility of information and its appropriateness in meeting their needs.
- Students should have the tools to critically evaluate their own and others' multimedia works.

NCTE Principles Regarding Assessment

The original version of this document, titled "Standards for the Assessment of Reading and Writing, Revised Edition (2009)," can be found on NCTE's website at http://www.ncte.org/standards/assessmentstandards. This document was authored by members of the Joint IRA–NCTE Task Force on Assessment, Peter Johnston (chair), Peter Afflerbach, Sandra Krist, Kathryn Mitchell Pierce, Elizabeth Spalding, Alfred W. Tatum, and Sheila W. Valencia.

Assessment is an integral part of instruction, and NCTE affirms its importance for student learning. In particular, formative assessment can be a powerful means of improving student achievement because it is assessment *for* learning, but it must adhere to key principles to be effective. These principles include emphasizing timely and task-focused feedback because it is feedback, not the absence of a grade, that characterizes effective formative assessment; shaping instructional decisions based on student performance in formative assessment; embedding formative assessment in instruction because the use of a given instrument of assessment, not the instrument itself, confers value on formative assessment; and offering students increased opportunities to understand their own learning. The principles below, developed in collaboration with the International Reading Association, suggest how assessment, both formative and summative, can enhance student achievement.

What we know about assessment:

- Assessment experiences at all levels, whether formative or summative, have consequences for students.
- Assessment should emphasize what students can do rather than what they cannot do.
- Assessment must provide useful information to inform and enable reflection.
- If any individual student's interests are not served by an assessment practice, regardless of whether it is intended for administration or decision making by an individual or by a group, then that practice is not valid for that student.
- The most productive and powerful assessments for students are likely to be the formative assessments that occur in the daily activities of the classroom.
- The teacher is the most important agent of assessment.
- Teachers need to feel safe to share, discuss, and critique their own work with others.
- Teacher knowledge cannot be replaced by standardized tests.
- The primary purpose of assessment is to improve teaching and learning.

What this means for teachers:

- Teachers should be able to demonstrate how their assessment practices benefit and do not harm individual students.
- Teachers must be aware of and deliberate about their roles as assessors.
- Teachers must have routines for systematic assessment to ensure that each student is benefiting optimally from instruction.
- Teacher leaders and administrators need to recognize that improving teachers' assessment expertise requires ongoing professional development, coaching, and access to professional learning communities. Nurturing such communities must be a priority for improving assessment.
- Teachers must take responsibility for making and sharing judgments about students' achievements and progress.
- Teachers should give students multiple opportunities to talk about their writing.
- Schools and teachers must develop a trusting relationship with the surrounding community.

Author

S usi Long is a professor of early childhood education and language and literacy at the University of South Carolina. Following a career as a classroom teacher, she completed her doctorate at The Ohio State University. For the past fifteen years, her work with children, teachers, and university students has focused on language and literacy learning across cultural and linguistic communities, the early years of teaching, equity pedagogies, and culturally relevant literacy practices.

Contributing Authors

William Hutchinson is a doctoral student in the Joint Program in English and Education at the University of Michigan, where he also teaches composition in the English department Writing Program. He has taught English and writing at various schools in both Boston, Massachusetts, and Dublin, Ireland. Hutchinson graduated with a degree in English and a Massachusetts State teaching license from the University of Massachusetts Boston and obtained a master's degree in Anglo-Irish literature and drama from University College Dublin, Ireland. He does research in literacy studies and adult education.

Justine Neiderhiser is a doctoral student in the Joint Program in English and Education at the University of Michigan. After completing a bachelor's degree in English at Millersville University and a master's degree in rhetoric and composition at North Carolina State University, she joined the English and Education program to pursue her interests in composition theory and pedagogy. As a writing instructor at both North Carolina State and Michigan, Neiderhiser has been particularly invested in helping her students develop transferrable skills that build on their prior knowledge. Her interest in writing instruction extends across grade levels, from the early acquisition of literacy to the college writing classroom.

More Contributing Authors

Vignette Authors: Clearly, the authors of the classroom vignettes in this book play an essential role as contributing authors. The teacher-authors were introduced at the beginning of each classroom snapshot (Meet the Teacher), but in some vignettes, university faculty shared the authoring role. We introduce them here:

Tasha Tropp Laman is an associate professor of language and literacy and elementary education at the University of South Carolina. Her work focuses on critical literacies in multilingual communities and takes her into the worlds of children and teachers in elementary classrooms every week. This commitment is foundational to her focus as a teacher educator and researcher.

Julia López-Robertson is an assistant professor of language and literacy at the University of South Carolina. Her vignette is written about her days as a classroom teacher. Today, she focuses her research and teaching on the intersections between language, race, ethnicity, and culture as they relate to the teaching and learning of emerging bilinguals. She considers time spent every week in early childhood classrooms as central to her role as a university faculty member.

Katie Van Sluys is an associate professor of literacy in the Department of Teacher Education at DePaul University. Her work focuses on the lives of multilingual learners, young writers, and teachers as they develop and enact their understandings of literacy in today and tomorrow's worlds. Her work grows from close, regular collaboration with Chicago schools, administrators, teachers, families, and elementary students.

This book was typeset in TheMix and Palatino by Precision Graphics.

The typeface used on the cover is Myriad Pro.

The book was printed on 60-lb. White Recycled Opaque Offset paper by Versa Press, Inc.

30% Total Recycled Fiber